On Architecture and Work

On Architecture and Work

The Political Economy of Space Vol. 3

HATJE CANTZ

Table of Contents

The Labor of Building

Charlotte Malterre-Barthes

> The silence about the amount of human labor invested in the production of built space is embarrassing.[1]—Katie Lloyd Thomas, Silke Kapp, and João Marcos Lopes

> Work, work, work, work, work, work[2]—Rihanna

What impact could prioritizing labor have on architectural work? In the context of the political economy of space (i.e., the processes through which space is produced, commodified, and controlled within capitalist systems), it requires setting aside the body of work—the oeuvre—to take instead stock of how much work building involves, whose bodies execute it, and what value it holds. "Work" defines "labor as a measurable commodity," whereas "labor" entails "physical effort" and refers to "services workers perform for wages"—Karl Marx's fundamental transaction of capitalism: wage labor, or the selling of labor power.[3] This exchange conceals exploitation, as workers produce more value than they receive in wages. Surplus value—the difference between what workers create and what they are paid—is appropriated by capital, in this case, real estate. Exploitation occurs across the spectrum, from the design office to the construction site, though in different forms and intensities.

Under capitalism, there is nothing special or new about that articulation. However, architecture shows a peculiar reserve regarding work as a fundamental aspect of space production—an unwillingness to address either the long hours spent on planning tasks, or the harsh working conditions on-site. This physical and ideological distance reveals itself in the divide between spaces of conception and spaces of execution, the office and the construction site.[4] Examining wage labor throughout the commodity chain of built space asks: Who labors for it, and at what cost?—from designing a project and organizing its fabrication, negotiating with contractors, assigning or assembling a team that will then execute the designs, demolishing or excavating, terracing the ground, sourcing and transporting construction materials, pouring concrete or installing appliances, mounting walls, painting, plastering, roofing, etc. These actions form a commodity chain "composed of a series of operations or transformations, a set of agents and a system of markets … as well as the behavior of the agents."[5] Thus, agents involved in space production include those who contribute directly and act upon transforming land into a built commodity, from the architectural worker to the construction site laborer.

The hand versus mind debate has long framed this divide. Some have argued that the *cosa mentale* is superior to the labor of the executants—a conceptualized vision requires hand labor to be realized; such an operation is only the means to an end: the intellectual labor, the idea, comes first.[6] This preposterous articulation justifies the hierarchical superiority of design work—namely, authority and authorship—over construction skills. It wrongly claims that the oeuvre exists purely through the design instructions. In recent decades, scholars like Peggy Deamer, Katie Lloyd Thomas, and Sérgio Ferro have expertly deconstructed these notions, paving the way for the current reflection.[7]

On Architecture and Work argues for continued political introspection on labor in architectural production. Both office and construction are representative spaces of exploitation and friction, where, paradoxically, the collective aspect of work is revealed. The equation can be complexified by admitting that the profoundly collective aspect of realizing a project within an architecture office is still obscured by liability mechanisms that require an individual to sign official documents and take responsibility, a system mirrored on the construction site, where hierarchies of skill also persist.[8]

A construction site remains a critical taboo in architecture: a dangerous and contentious place filled with potential liability. In many countries, punishments for infractions of safety responsibilities include jail time and a ban on practice for architects.[9] One can freely criticize a rendering or a completed building, but rarely an ongoing operation, as if the in-process aspect of the construction site and its inherent risks rendered it invisible, subtracted from opinion. The discursive visibility of the construction site is inversely proportional to its centrality in our discipline. Yet it contains layers of profound meaning about how architecture materializes and how societies function. It is a landing point for capital and the social division of work, and as such, a crucial entry point to reassessing the position of labor in the commodity chain of space production.

As Manfredo Tafuri, Douglas Spencer, Mariella d'Aprile, and others have articulated, a class divide separates architects as intellectual laborers from construction workers performing manual labor under precarious conditions, with little solidarity between them.[10] Both groups face hardship: the architecture office perpetuates exploitation through unpaid internships and overtime, while construction workers face precarious employment, dangerous on-site conditions, and systematic devaluation of their contributions to the built environment. Impatient capital is prescribed through a complex web of forces: returns and interest rates, rigid

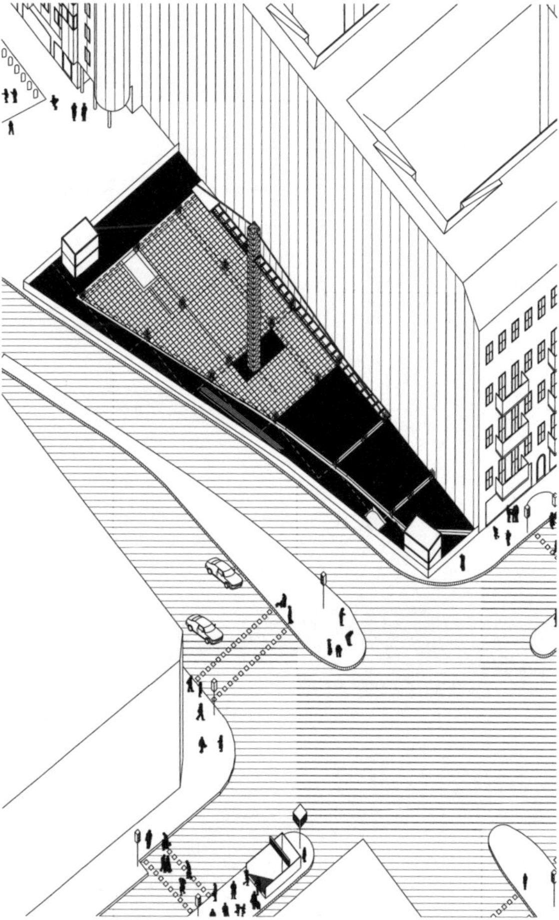

Axonometric view of the construction site for a tourist boarding house at Hermannstraße 227, Berlin (fall 2018, TU Berlin, Davide Broggio, Valentina Nadwornicek, Sofia Vila Clavell)

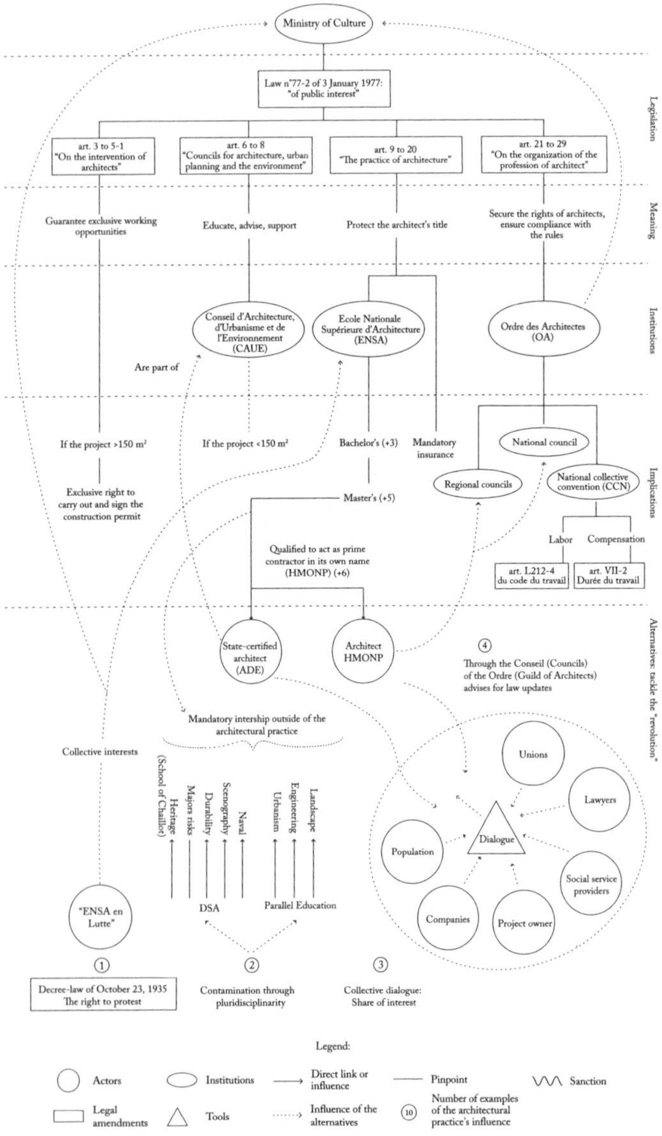
Ministry of Culture
Legislation
Law n°77-2 of 3 January 1977: "of public interest"
art. 3 to 5-1 "On the intervention of architects"
art. 6 to 8 "Councils for architecture, urban planning and the environment"
art. 9 to 20 "The practice of architecture"
art. 21 to 29 "On the organization of the profession of architect"
Meaning
Guarantee exclusive working opportunities
Educate, advise, support
Protect the architect's title
Secure the rights of architects, ensure compliance with the rules
Institutions
Conseil d'Architecture, d'Urbanisme et de l'Environnement (CAUE)
Ecole Nationale Supérieure d'Architecture (ENSA)
Ordre des Architectes (OA)
Are part of
Implications
If the project >150 m²
If the project <150 m²
Bachelor's (+3)
Mandatory insurance
National council
Regional councils
National collective convention (CCN)
Exclusive right to carry out and sign the construction permit
Master's (+5)
Qualified to act as prime contractor in its own name (HMONP) (+6)
Labor
Compensation
art. L212-4 du code du travail
art. VII-2 Durée du travail
Alternatives: tackle the "revolution"
State-certified architect (ADE)
Architect HMONP
4
Through the Conseil (Councils) of the Ordre (Guild of Architects) advises for law updates
Mandatory intership outside of the architectural practice
Collective interests
Heritage (School of Chaillot)
Majors risks
Durability
Scenography
Naval
Urbanism
Engineering
Landscape
DSA
Parallel Education
Unions
Lawyers
Population
Dialogue
Social service providers
Companies
Project owner
"ENSA en Lutte"
1
Decree-law of October 23, 1935 The right to protest
2
Contamination through pluridisciplinarity
3
Collective dialogue: Share of interest
Legend:
Actors
Institutions
Direct link or influence
Pinpoint
Sanction
Legal amendments
Tools
Influence of the alternatives
10
Number of examples of the architectural practice's influence

Architects' drafting office during construction of the
Sydney Opera House (1963, Don McPhedran for the Australian
Photographic Agency, the State Library, NSW)
Left: Regulations for French architectural practice
(2024, Eva Oustric, RIOT/ EPFL)

The labor of construction (2025, Charlotte Malterre-Barthes)

completion dates, risk-averse insurers, and pressures to avoid delay penalties, to name a few.

This volume, *On Architecture and Work*, following *On Architecture and Greenwashing* and *On Architecture and the Greenfield*, is the third in The Political Economy of Space series. It assembles essays by practitioners, theorists, workers, and activists, exploring the deep-seated narratives of labor, design, and economics.[11] It seeks to shed light on the distance between design and construction and to articulate this gap as a space of friction that could be productive if occupied further. The contributions emerged from "Work—Architecture and Labor," a lecture series hosted by the RIOT laboratory at the Swiss Federal Institute of Technology-EPFL during the "Fix the Office" design studio (spring 2024).[12] Taking construction sites as starting points, the studio examined how architects generate economic value, and how they might redesign exploitative business models to address today's looming social and climate emergencies.[13] Investigating power dynamics in offices, financial and legal frameworks of the profession globally, billing schemes, and labor conditions to uncover the causality between operative ways and built work, the studio explored how an office's business model, status, and institutional framework impact the architecture it generates, and how these structures can be edited for a post-extractive practice.[14] The design task focused on creating alternatives forms of world-making—of "not being an office," while confronting uncomfortable questions about the value of architecture, with actual construction sites as spaces of intervention.[15]

Four essays insist that labor—its conditions, value, and organization—should be central to architectural discourse. They demonstrate that labor questions are fundamentally architectural questions, not distractions. The buildings we design are inseparable from their production conditions—in the office or on-site.

In "For Solidaristic Practices in Architectural Work," critic Marisa Cortright introduces the figure of the "Architectural Killjoy," a powerful role model who disrupts comfortable narratives about the profession, calling for broader solidarity among architectural workers across geographical and professional boundaries.[16] In conversation with (non-)Swiss Architects, she examines how organizing efforts are emerging across Europe, particularly among foreign architectural workers facing exploitation that is compounded by precarious immigration status.

Labor researcher and architect Namita Vijay Dharia, in "The Architecture of Collectivity," reports from construction sites in India's National Capital Region through the testimonies of Ahmed, Mahaab, and Omprakash—workers whose intelligence, entrepreneurial spirit, and design capabilities challenge the industry's hierarchical dismissal of their potential.[17] Through ethnographic research, Dharia reveals how labor, love, and skill intersect in construction practices, exposing both exploitation and untapped creative potential.

"The Union, the Insurance, and the Workers: Voices from the Construction Site," compiled by architecture students Carolina Pichler and Lalie Porteret, brings forward voices from Swiss construction sites through interviews with union representatives, insurance officials, and on-site workers, demonstrating that even in a country with good labor protections, the relentless pace of construction mercilessly extracts value from workers' bodies.

The final essay, "Architecture, Politics and Self-Management," by Brazilian collective Usina-CTAH with Pedro Fiori Arantes, presents a radical way of engaging design labor and construction through the Brazilian *mutirão* model—a self-managed construction process in which future residents collectively build their housing with the technical support of designers and public funds. This contribution, inspired by the work of the TF/TK group (Translating Ferro / Transforming Knowledges of Architecture, Design and Labour for the New Field of Production Studies), translates an essay originally written in Portuguese and presents an example of what solidarity between architectural and construction workers can be and the kind of architecture it produces.[18]

The 2024 scaffolding collapse on a Swiss construction site that killed three workers, as documented by Pichler and Porteret, and the wrenching testimonies of Dharia's investigation on the construction sites of the National Capital Region, remind us that construction workers remain the most vulnerable population in the "supply chain of space production." This publication hopes to bring invisible labor into the foreground—whether involved with Swiss construction sites, Indian urban developments, European architecture offices, or Brazilian *mutirões*—to contribute to reform movements within the field and forge connections with broader labor struggles. Confronting architecture's labor question is essential to creating a less extractive, more just built environment.[19] Articulating architecture as the result of a sum of commodities plus labor power turned into another commodity—space—and rethinking systems that fuel bodily exhaustion, social devastation, environmental depletion, and capital accumulation are essential stepping stones toward identifying leverage points for an insurgent design practice.

1 Katie Lloyd Thomas, Silke Kapp, and João Marcos Lopes, "Preface," *Architecture from Below: An Anthology* (London: MACK, 2024).
2 Rihanna, "Work," Ritter / Graham / Brathwaite / Moir / Samuels / Fenty / Thomas © Monte

Moir Music, Sony / ATV Music Publishing LLC, Universal Music Publishing Group, Warner Chappell Music, Inc.

3 See Karl Marx, *A Contribution to the Critique of Political Economy* (New York: International Publishers, 1970).

4 To be fair, in small firms, this division is less pronounced, with a project often being guided during its execution phase by the same architect who designs, plans, and supervises the work, appearing on-site once a week to ensure that everything is proceeding according to their plans. In larger firms, however, construction leadership tasks are typically alienated, and assigned to a specialized team or outsourced. Moreover, throughout the profession, the materialization of design through labor is seldom considered during design processes, unless it directly affects costs for the client.

5 Fabien Tallec and Louis Bockel, "Commodity Chain Analysis: Constructing the Commodity Chain Functional Analysis and Flow Charts," *Rome: UN Food and Agriculture Organization*, (2005), p. 2.

6 Anne Dujin, "Introduction," *Esprit* 1–2 (2025).

7 Peggy Deamer, *Architecture and Labor* (London: Routledge, 2020); Katie Lloyd Thomas, Tilo Amhoff, and Nick Beech, eds., *Industries of Architecture*, Critiques 11 (London: Routledge, 2016); Sérgio Ferro, *Architecture from Below: An Anthology*, trans. Ellen Heyward and Ana Naomi de Sousa, Silvia Kapp and Mariana Moura, eds. (London: MACK, 2024); Jakob Walter et al., "Formalizing Work Relationships in Architecture Firms," in *ARCH+, The Business of Architecture* (Leipzig/Berlin: Spector Books, 2024).

8 Gauthier Bolle, Maxime Decommer, and Valérie Nègre, "The Architect's Office: Practice and Organization of Work (18th–21st Century)," *Les Cahiers de la recherche architecturale urbaine et paysagère* 9 (2020).

9 Le Premier ministre, "Code de Déontologie des Architectes," in *Décret n°80-217 du 20 mars 1980 portant code des devoirs professionnels des architectes*, ed. République Française (Paris: Journal Officiel de la République Française, 1980); see also https://www.legifrance.gouv.fr/codes/texte_lc/LEGITEXT000006074232/.

10 Marianela D'Aprile and Douglas Spencer, "Notes on Tafuri, Militancy, and Unionization," *The Avery Review* 56 (2022), https://averyreview.com/issues/56/notes-on-tafuri (accessed April 24, 2025).

11 Charlotte Malterre-Barthes, ed., *On Architecture and Greenwashing*, The Political Economy of Space Vol. 01 (Berlin: Hatje Cantz Verlag, 2024); idem, ed., *On Architecture and the Greenfield*, The Political Economy of Space Vol. 02 (Berlin: Hatje Cantz Verlag, 2024).

12 RIOT stands for Research and Innovation On architecture, urban design and Territory laboratory. "Fix the Office" refers to the title of a chapter from Charlotte Malterre-Barthes, *A Moratorium on New Construction*, Critical Spatial Practice 14 (London: Sternberg Press, 2025), as well as the eponymous studio: https://riot.today/spring-2024-a-moratorium-on-new-construction-fix-the-office/ (accessed April 24, 2025).

13 Investigating construction sites has long been part of my pedagogy. Studios taught on Cairo's self-built settlements (ETHZ, 2014–17) tackled processes, sites, materials, and labor, while the studio "Political Spaces" (TU Berlin, 2018–19), and more recently the workshop "Construction as Site" (Politecnico di Milano, 2025), challenged ongoing construction sites.

14 ROSCA: Rotating Savings and Credit Associations, ZAD: Zone A Défendre.

15 See results on EPFL's Living Archives website: https://livingarchives.epfl.ch/projects/?type=Collection&year=2024&academic=Spring&unit=RIOT&sort

=date%E2%96%BC&collection=1157 (accessed April 24, 2025).

16 See also Marisa Cortright, *"Can This Be? Surely This Cannot Be?" Architectural Workers Organizing in Europe* (Prague: VI PER Gallery, 2021).

17 See also Namita Vijay Dharia, *The Industrial Ephemeral: Labor and Love in Indian Architecture and Construction* (Berkely: University of California Press, 2022).

18 The group's efforts in translating Sérgio Ferro's work, which articulates the relationship between materials, labor exploitation, and construction, hold significant value and influence for this publication. See https://tftk.iau.usp.br/en/ (accessed April 24, 2025); see also Pedro Fiori Arantes, *The Rent of Form: Architecture and Labor in the Digital Age*, trans. Adriana Kauffmann (Minneapolis: University of Minnesota Press, 2019).

19 Some of these thoughts have been previously articulated and published. See Charlotte Malterre-Barthes, "Architecture of Extraction," in Justinian Tribillon et al., eds., *Visible Upon Breakdown: Exploring the Cultural, Political, and Spatial Nature of Infrastructure* (Berlin: Spector 2024); Charlotte Malterre-Barthes, "Carbon Architecture: Toward an Expanded Political Economy of Space Production," in Jeffrey Huang et al., eds., *Transcalar Prospects in Climate Crisis: Architectural Research in Re/action* (Basel: Lars Müller Publishers, 2024); and Malterre-Barthes, A *Moratorium* (see note 12).

For Solidaristic Practices in Architectural Work

Marisa Cortright

The Architectural Killjoy

If I were to summarize the role that I had in an office job at an architectural company, it would be that of an Architectural Killjoy—a figure grounded in Sara Ahmed's *Feminist Killjoy,* who kills the joy of, or causes problems for, other feminists.[1] The Architectural Killjoy is the architect who kills the joy of other architects. Even now, the independent work I'm doing as a writer, researcher, and editor is killing architects' joy by inciting critical analysis of architectural production.

In 2018, a friend from graduate school and I put together a proposal for the Architecture Fringe Festival in Scotland. We called our proposal *Architect Killjoys,* invoking Ahmed and the feeling propelled by what was then a new phenomenon, the "Shitty Architecture Men List," a spreadsheet where anonymous contributors shared experiences of harassment and abuse by powerful men in architecture.[2] We advertised for a bar gathering where we could air criticism of the industry's institutions and practices. Yet either because of the way we advertised the gathering (with snippets from the Shitty Architecture Men List) or because no one felt it was necessary, or wanted to be seen attending such an event, no one showed up. At the time, I was disappointed, but in retrospect, I think that's the life of the Killjoy—the sound of crickets chirping around you.

Fortunately, later that year, I had the experience of seeing someone more powerful than me model what it would look like to be an Architectural Killjoy when someone is actually listening. The architectural historian Aaron Betsky gave a talk at a party hosted by my employer to celebrate the World Architecture Festival in Amsterdam, an annual event that attracted the company's consultants and clients. Betsky advocated a halt to new construction, arguing that architects should drastically shift their energy toward renovating existing buildings. During the talk, the company's owner smiled along. Later, he expressed his displeasure with Betsky's message. Betsky had killed some major joy, indeed. Even though I'm not speaking to the owners of architectural companies when I write and talk, I do try to channel Betsky's willingness to upset a party or a client.

Recently, I was on a selection committee for the architect-in-residence program at the Amsterdam Centre for Architecture (ARCAM). Many applications included a budget with insignificant honoraria for speakers in ARCAM's public programming. In our jury session, I commented, "If this applicant is going to receive the residency, they're going to have to adjust their budget to respect the labor of the people they're inviting to work with them." The person running the jury session replied dismissively, "Of course, you think that. That's your thing," because I've written about architectural workers and the need to compensate them fairly for their work. If I'd pushed my Killjoy sensibilities further, I would have responded that ARCAM needs to make paying people for their work *their* thing. Killjoys do this: they insist on making their thing the thing of others. Ahmed describes how, when the Feminist Killjoy points out a problem, they are subsequently identified as the problem. In other words, the difficulty shifts from the difficult thing (being underpaid) to the person saying it is difficult, the Killjoy. Judging by how no one showed up to our Architect Killjoy event in Scotland, it can be lonely to inhabit the role of the Architectural Killjoy.

However, finding peers who share your misgivings and with whom you feel comfortable discussing them can be really encouraging. The office job I used to have involved communication and business development. It was architectural overhead work—not billed directly to the client. It's the kind of job that can be held by someone who studied architecture but isn't necessarily the job of someone who is trained in architecture. It's the kind of job that doesn't require more than the contractually agreed forty or however many hours per week. The longer that I worked in this job, both alongside and in close collaboration with architects who worked more than their contractually agreed number of hours per week, the more sharply I felt a divide between those working in administrative positions like me, and those working in architect positions, even interns. The latter shared several misgivings with me. For instance, we wondered, "Why is there so much unpaid labor in this office? Why are we working on these kinds of projects? Why are we working with these kinds of clients?" And yet we seemed to lack the will or the ability to channel those misgivings into the Killjoy's critique.

This divide between overhead workers and architectural workers is the subject of my 2019 article, "Death to the Calling: A Job in Architecture Is Still a Job."[3] "Calling" refers to the mystical faith in one's relationship to architecture, which downplays the significance of hurdles encountered in studying or working simply because one is "called" to be an architect. I identified this divide as a barrier to non-architects and architects finding common ground and organizing together to address their misgivings. I also cited the efforts of a group of people in the UK who called themselves architectural workers and later formed the Section of Architectural Workers (SAW) union in 2020. They initially organized against unpaid overtime, salaries below living wages, and unfair treatment and discrimination in the workplace. They were the first instance I had seen of people working in architecture organizing specifically as architectural workers. Inspired by SAW, I wrote a book of short essays titled *"Can This Be? Surely This Cannot Be?" Architectural Workers Organizing in Europe.*[4]

Architectural Workers

Who are architectural workers? Why refer to them as such? What do I mean by organizing? And organizing for what? I understood Europe as a political project that controls labor flows in all kinds of work, including architectural work, and used it as the geographical boundary for the book. I interviewed union members and people working in different positions who are organizing in different spaces, including academic groups like the TU Delft Feminists, Claiming Spaces, and the Future Architects Front, as well as a moderator of the Instagram account Dank Lloyd Wright.[5] My interviewees described how their careers and lives had been shaped by the forces of the EU, or rather, the "freedom" of movement of labor that nationals of EU member countries are granted to work in other member countries, a freedom that was foreclosed for British nationals following Brexit.

For foreign architectural workers in the EU and non-EU nationals, the "freedom" to move can become a compulsion, depending on how the market is working. Architectural workers from Southern European countries like Spain, Portugal, Greece, or Italy leave because there is not enough dignified architectural work for the number of qualified architects. Keyword: dignified. I'm putting scare quotes around "freedom" because the seeming smoothness of Europe's open borders for EU passport holders comes with an inverse hardening of Europe's borders for the others—most obviously, refugees who are fleeing perilous circumstances, namely in Africa and the Middle East, to come to Europe, but also workers from countries outside the EU who come for labor reasons. For those workers, the ordeal of living and working in the EU, and in Switzerland, as a border regime, has been made intentionally onerous to discourage labor immigration, on the one hand, and on the other hand, to discipline the labor that does make it into the country.

An anonymous group called Foreign Architects Switzerland (FAS) published a zine in 2012 that took to task the idea that employed architects in Switzerland have it easy by virtue of working in such a rich country.[6] It asks, "Is the idea of an architectural proletariat a joke? Why do you complain about your salary? Are Swiss-employed architects spoiled bastards?"[7] Most crucially, for me,

Zine #4, Foreign Architects Switzerland, 2012

the zine puts forward the claim that "it's not because it's worse elsewhere that you should accept bad at home."[8]

I took that forward into 2022 when I wrote "It Could Always Be Worse" for *ARCH+*.[9] I based the piece on interviews with architectural workers in German-speaking countries—Germany, Austria, and Switzerland—who had originally come from the southeastern periphery of Europe, primarily from former Yugoslavia, the Czech Republic, and Romania.[10] I argue that FAS's claim to not accept bad at home because it's worse elsewhere "chimes with the cause of architectural workers organizing in the US and Europe, who insist that it's not because it's worse in other industries that architectural workers should accept bad conditions in architecture."[11] Among organizing spaces in architecture, we frequently hear that "the architects who organize as professionalized workers, who are white-collar workers, are relatively well-off." And that may be true, but that's no reason to stop and wait until everyone else has gotten to where architectural workers are.

A similar claim about immigrant workers could also be made. For instance, for the architectural workers who come from countries where there's no minimum wage or protections for workers, or where architects take on huge amounts of liability and an excessive number of projects, we need to thread these two assertions together. Immigrant architectural workers have the right to complain as immigrants and as workers. Depending on their visa status, their situation may be incredibly precarious, even if they earn more money and have better working conditions than they would have in their country of origin. In one of my interviews, a woman called Katarina from Serbia described how "when applying for a visa in Germany, one needs to earn a certain amount per hour, which is the government's way of ensuring that a worker can live off their salary." For many architecture firms, this is too much to pay, especially for junior architects. So, to fulfill the requirement, several Berlin offices give out fake thirty-hour contracts. In reality, those employees work full-time. Unfortunately, the fake thirty-hour contracts are well known among immigrant architects who are not from the EU. The sad part is that in many cases, the EU workers also get the same low salary, and "when non-EU workers work forty-plus hour work weeks, but are only paid for thirty hours, that devalues not only their labor but all of their coworkers' labor as well."

The main assertion of this *ARCH+* piece is that German, Austrian, and Swiss architectural workers would do best to recognize the plight of their immigrant colleagues and organize together with them against the discrimination they face as immigrants and as workers.

I insist on the necessity of solidaristic practices in architectural work. These practices extend beyond what we consider to be the bounds of architectural work and workplaces. They are of an internationalist nature and reject the views of regimes imposed, for instance, by the EU. They are practices that attempt to counter the competitive nature of architectural education and private practice.

Vitruvius Grind's *Welcome to the Grind: A Guide for New and Recent Architecture School Graduates* is an example of solidaristic practice. It acknowledges that working in architecture is a "grind" while displaying a generosity of spirit, which is exceptionally rare in architectural spaces.[12] It confronts the idea that grinding is the only way to operate in architecture. Put another way, the attitudes "because I've suffered, other people should suffer too" and "it wouldn't be fair not to suffer as an architectural worker," are not ones that we should take forward. Rather, we need to confront them head-on with models that offer alternative approaches, like this guide.[13]

Kate Wagner's "A Wall of Silence," published in the *New York Review of Architecture* (NYRA) in the fall of 2023, is also an example calling for solidaristic practices in architectural work.[14] Wagner asks, "Why don't architects have anything to say about Gaza?" She makes the point that she can

Welcome to the Grind: A Guide for New and Recent Architecture School Graduates, Vitruvius Grind, June 8, 2022

write essays challenging the status quo, regardless of whether there is someone who pays her to do that, but "creating architecture is different because its practice is almost entirely tied to capital, power, and money. As a result, it can never subvert those systems because it needs them to survive."[15] She's quick to add that the field being held hostage by shock capitalism and imperialism is not an excuse for practitioners to throw up their hands, but rather a call for practitioners to at least use their voices to take a stand. "In the case of Palestine," she suggests, "organization at the firm level to pressure employers to boycott projects in Gaza would be a good step."[16] I agree. The power of architectural workers organizing refusal to cooperate in further colonizing Palestine is as yet untapped. Evoking the figure of the architectural comrade, we can think about how architect-organized architectural workers could direct their power in concert with other workers outside the architectural sector.

Allow me to turn to the US, whose government has made possible the Israeli bombing of Gaza. In the NYRA last fall, I wrote "Better Bargain," a piece about the state of architectural workers organizing in the US.[17] In the last few years, much of that organizing in the private sector has been conducted under the umbrella of Architectural Workers United (AWU), a campaign that came out of the ultimately unsuccessful attempt to form a union at SHoP Architects in New York. AWU operates as a connector between workers at private firms who want to unionize and the International Association of Machinists and Aerospace Workers (the Machinists). In addition to the handful of architecture firms that have been unionized by AWU, the Machinists are also the union that represents a number of weapons and military contractors. These are the same companies supplying the fighter jets and bombs with which Israel is bombing Gaza.[18] I mention this because we can't form a just internationalist vision of architectural production unless we pay attention to the way in which we organize. In what kinds of unions do we organize? Alongside which non-architectural comrades do we organize? And while some architectural workers may feel comfortable forming unions solely for the purpose of improving their salaries and their working conditions, it is the architectural comrades who connect the improvement of their salaries and working conditions to international struggles for justice that extend beyond what they build, and beyond what they consider to be properly "architectural." They are those who might be able to bring some weight to bear on the US government and its support for the Israeli regime of genocide. In short, how we organize in no small part determines the limits or the expanses of what we can organize for.

I'll close by mentioning a piece recently published in *The Avery Review*.[19] In 2023, I was their guest editor and commissioned an essay from the Alternative

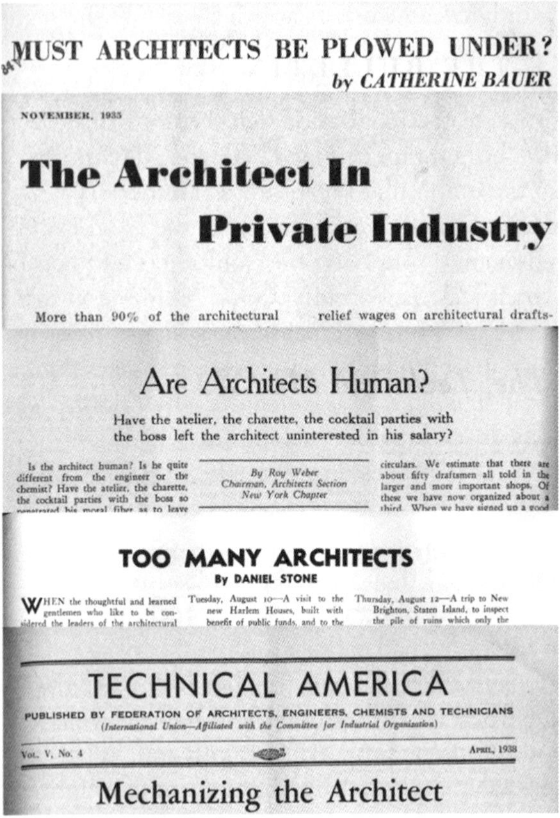
MUST ARCHITECTS BE PLOWED UNDER?

by CATHERINE BAUER

NOVEMBER, 1935

The Architect In Private Industry

More than 90% of the architectural

relief wages on architectural drafts-

Are Architects Human?

Have the atelier, the charette, the cocktail parties with the boss left the architect uninterested in his salary?

Is the architect human? Is he quite different from the engineer or the chemist? Have the atelier, the charette, the cocktail parties with the boss so

By Roy Weber
Chairman, Architects Section
New York Chapter

circulars. We estimate that there are about fifty draftsmen all told in the larger and more important shops. Of these we have now organized about a third.

TOO MANY ARCHITECTS

By DANIEL STONE

WHEN the thoughtful and learned gentlemen who like to be con-

Tuesday, August 10—A visit to the new Harlem Houses, built with

Thursday, August 12—A trip to New Brighton, Staten Island, to inspect

TECHNICAL AMERICA

PUBLISHED BY FEDERATION OF ARCHITECTS, ENGINEERS, CHEMISTS AND TECHNICIANS
(International Union—Affiliated with the Committee for Industrial Organization)

VOL. V, No. 4 APRIL, 1938

Mechanizing the Architect

Various 1930s headlines about the figure of the architect, collected by Joshua Barnett, Adare Brown, James Heard, Jack Rusk, and the Alternative Building Industry Collective, 2024

Building Industry Collective, based in New York. The essay describes a publication called *The Bulletin,* produced by the Federation of Architects, Engineers, Chemists, and Technicians (FAECT), a Depression-era union of technical workers. *The Bulletin* charted FAECT's efforts to win "bread-and-butter" concessions, like a living-wage salary for their members, and also attempted to change public policy. They wanted to ameliorate how the US government administered the New Deal programs, namely focusing on better flood control to manage environmental catastrophes and the construction of new public housing. They did so by closing ranks among professionalized workers in various technical trades. They created a title called "technical worker," which lumped everyone—architects, engineers, chemists, technicians—together. And while the silos that separate architects from engineers from technicians today are perhaps much greater than they were then, seeking such comradely bonds between similar professions could mark an important step towards architectural workers finding solidarity outside of architecture, towards considering more broadly the full expanse of architectural production.

Q&A

Beatrice Meloni (BM), (non-)Swiss Architects

We non-Swiss architects are not a minority. In Zurich, around 50% of the people working in architecture firms are foreigners: people with migrant backgrounds, internal migrants from other cantons, or even people with non-Swiss-sounding names experience similar problems.[20] Exploitative labor conditions affect Swiss and other workers. Starting from our claims and requests, we can mobilize together. We cannot change the impact of our practice on society if we don't start from the work ethics inside the office. At the same time, we need to face an unresolved issue: How can we ask the underdogs—unrecognized non-Swiss architects—to be the protagonists of a change in the architecture sector in Switzerland? For example, women bring important reflections from inside architecture—in academia and practice—but are often unheard. How can we face the desire to be the protagonist, knowing that we struggle to get legitimacy inside our own working world and in our political actions?

Marisa Cortright (MC)

It's worth reflecting on the fact that around 50% of architectural workers in Zurich—a nucleus of architectural work and the country—come from elsewhere and are already legitimate protagonists in their latent potential to be organized.

So, my Killjoy reaction is to say, "Don't look for it in the first place. Activate those 50% of people into work. Keep working adjacent to and with an eye on what legitimized institutions are doing, but don't seek recognition from them." Further, I doubt institutional legitimacy: If we're seeking a new set of values, a new ethic for architecture, can we judge our numbers or strategies based on other existing institutions' ethics? Workers must supersede the realm of legitimacy through their own means. They must make these kinds of bodies irrelevant by pushing them out of the position of the protagonist—not by replicating what they've done, not by seeking representation in their bodies by becoming certified architects, but instead by creating new forms of legitimacy. Yet, it's difficult to say what those look like in different geographies or localities.

Enzo Nercolini (EN)

(Non-)Swiss Architects doesn't yet have institutional recognition. It's our long-term goal to achieve that mass to have bargaining power collectively. There have been efforts to unionize, but no substantial wins in the recent past. The digital world and social media have made it easier for non-institutionalized communities to achieve some recognition from the public. At (non-)Swiss Architects, we build that grassroots informational base, aiming for solidarity, learning about the problems in the industry, and recognizing them as part of the workers' movement. But should we reach out to the Swiss equivalent of the Architects Chambers (e.g., the Swiss Society of Engineers and Architects, SIA)? From our perspective, these institutions are not there right now. They defend the interests of the owners. Often, in the history of unionizing movements, actual unions have become, over time, corporate activists who cease to defend the interests of the base because they have been consumed with their own internal workings and their institutionalization through the state. Lydia Hughes and Jamie Woodcock's book *Troublemaking*, while not aimed at architects, can assist anyone wondering about the benefits and complications that may arise from trying to organize in a workplace.[21]

MC

From my understanding, Switzerland has many small offices, and many people work in very small offices. So, when we think of "just talk to your coworkers," you might not have many coworkers who aren't your boss, right? How do you build bargaining power? Who are the other workers in your workplace? How do you gather when the workforce is scattered across more workplaces?

BM

In a way, we have become one of the main interlocutors for people experiencing bad workplace situations; we collect a lot of testimonies, people telling their stories or asking for salary advice, etc. Official Swiss organizations mostly support employers or regulate the associate-client relationship. There are some collective labor agreements in some cantons, but no direct support for the employees. An important part of our work is to give support, especially to foreign architectural workers who don't know the context and come with many questions. Some eventually join our group.

EN

While some of us have activated bargaining processes in the workplace, empowered by the collective support offered by our group, (non-) Swiss Architects is mostly composed of people who have been through some exploitative experiences as foreign workers. We still have to build a career as a group fighting for workers' rights.

MC

This sounds familiar to me. How can we discuss problems and solve them amongst ourselves? I'd like to leave it with one final thought: As part of Architecture Lobby's *Architecture Beyond Capitalism School*, I organized a session to think about how we keep relations with people who share our ethics for what architectural work could be—called "We Good?." We did it online, bringing together people who are geographically dispersed. Trying to find ways to create small online communities, Zoom could be a useful format. When you're thinking, "When we're not all together in person, how are we going to keep these solidarities together?," think about ways of tending to, caring for the solidarities with other people in architecture that you have.

1 Sara Ahmed, *The Feminist Killjoy Handbook* (London: Allen Lane, 2023).
2 "Shitty Architecture Men List," 2017, https://docs.google.com/spreadsheets/d/140sRIqK3D4IIcH33nrn3V7VENncfCQ1gFlu-1fIY1tM/edit?usp=sharing (accessed January 30, 2025). [the spreadsheet has been closed after the authors were pressured with legal consequence.—Ed.]
3 Marisa Cortright, "Death to the Calling: A Job in Architecture Is Still a Job," *Failed Architecture*, August 15, 2019, https://failedarchitecture.com/death-to-the-calling-a-job-in-architecture-is-still-a-job/ (accessed February 26, 2025).
4 Marisa Cortright, *"Can This Be? Surely This Cannot Be?" Architectural Workers Organizing in Europe* (Prague: VI PER Gallery, 2021).
5 In addition to these interviews, I also refer to literary and academic works such as Ivo Andrić, *The Bridge on the Drina*, trans. Lovett F. Edwards (New York: New York Review of Books, 1977).
6 Foreign Architects Switzerland, "Architectural Exploitation No More: Call to Unity," *FAS Zine* 4 (2012).
7 *FAS Zine* 4 (see note 6).
8 *FAS Zine* 4 (see note 6).
9 Marisa Cortright, "It Could Always Be Worse: Professional Migration in Architectural Sector," in: *ARCH+* et al., eds., *The Business of Architecture* (Leipzig/Berlin: Spector Books, 2024).
10 The term "German-speaking core" and "southeastern periphery" of Europe are terms coined by the author.

11 Cortright, "It Could Always Be Worse" (see note 10).
12 Vitruvius Grind, *Welcome to the Grind: A Guide for New and Recent Architectural School Graduates* (self-published, 2022).
13 The author, the anonymous Vitruvius Grind, is explicit about their wish for the guide to be widely shared, with the caveat that their work, and the work of the many contributors that they invited to share in it, is properly credited. It's a great example of how to model proper crediting and accreditation of other people's labor.
14 Kate Wagner, "A Wall of Silence," *New York Review of Architecture* 38/39 (November /December 2023, January/February 2024), https://nyra.nyc/articles/a-wall-of-silence (accessed February 27, 2025).
15 Wagner, "A Wall of Silence" (see note 14).
16 Wagner, "A Wall of Silence" (see note 14).
17 Marisa Cortright, "Better Bargain," *New York Review of Architecture* 37 (October 2023), https://nyra.nyc/articles/better-bargain-us-architecture-unions (accessed February 27, 2025).
18 These include Boeing, Lockheed Martin, and General Dynamics.
19 Alternative Building Industry Collective, "Our Best Organizer," *The Avery Review* 66 (March 2024), https://averyreview.com/issues/66/our-best-organizer (accessed February 27, 2025).
20 City of Zurich, *Swiss Earnings Structure for Architects in the City of Zurich 2018 (NOGA)* (October 2021).
21 Lydia Hughes and Jamie Woodcock, *Troublemaking* (London/New York: Verso, 2023).

An Architecture of Collectivity

Namita Vijay Dharia

A dump truck makes its way down the excavation pit at the Wandering Woods construction site on the outskirts of India's National Capital Region (NCR). The enormous pit, three stories deep and nearly the size of a football field, houses the growing foundations of a commercial real-estate complex. The construction site is surrounded by several other large sites in various stages of construction; the region hums with construction activity.

It is 2012, and my ethnographic research on NCR's construction industry brings me to the site. I stand inside the pit surrounded by bustling activity. It is a hot summer morning in May, and the mud walls of the pit shimmer in the heat. Work is at its peak. Small groups of workers, or teams, focus on different aspects of construction. Groups of Malda men and women carry mud in large *taslas* balanced on their heads.[1] Steelworkers construct the formwork for the foundations, the warp and weft of steel creating sculptural metal trees. Another team tamps down the mud floor of the pit using compactors and rollers, while layout masons begin to mark the lines and starters for new foundations. Each team is overseen by their foremen, who are in turn supervised by floor supervisors.

Jitendraji, the head site supervisor, stands in the pit today, and emotions run high as everyone strives to impress him.[2] Workers hammer with vigor or meticulously remeasure markings, while others move more quickly than usual. Supervisors bark instructions to show their attentiveness. The intensity of the atmosphere is heightened by the surrounding environment: the loud mechanical noises, the sparks from the welding machine, the clouds of dust, and the shouts and screams. All capped by the harsh, forty-nine-degree-Celsius heat that refuses to relent.

The steel radiates heat as Chaurasiya, Imran, and Nandu manipulate a column back into alignment. Their heads are wrapped in scarves for protection against the searing sun, but their hands remain exposed and raw. Chaurasiya wrenches hard at the formwork. His body lurches into the column, and I can feel his strength meet the might of the steel and plywood. The sun is so strong that I feel faint, yet the men continue to work. They, like everyone else in the pit, keep an eye out for the boy who carries water back and forth. When the young man arrives, Chaurasiya grabs a bottle and gulps down the water, letting it wash over his scorched hands and face.

The construction site is a realm of exceptional physical labor that demands both presence and wit. To build is to work exposed to the elements, often under extreme conditions, and one slipup can result in injury or even death. Construction requires not only physical strength but also intelligence, vigilance, and unwavering focus.

Work on construction sites transcends the boundaries between physical and mental labor; to labor in construction is to use mind and body to create the architectures in which many of us thrive. As growing calls to discuss the labor of architecture and the labor of architects arise, I examine the critiques and insights of construction workers who build the very structures we design and inhabit.[3] I present commentaries from three different construction workers within India's National Capital Region. Collectively, their experiences highlight the inequities and injustices that permeate the production chain of architecture while also revealing the untapped potential and skills that exist among workers in the industry. This raises a call for architects, developers, and contractors to think through new collective structures of production and design in architecture.

Ahmed

Ahmed, a young Tremix contractor at the Wandering Woods construction site, grew up in the rural areas of Chhattisgarh, India. He is the son of a *darzi* (tailor), a profession that falls under castes eligible for affirmative action due to their marginalized economic and social status. Ahmed's childhood was mired in discrimination and poverty. As the second of eight siblings, Ahmed loved to study and was top of his class. However, the embarrassment he experienced and the beatings he endured for not having proper clothing and school supplies made him leave school in the fifth grade. His family was too poor to support his intellectual pursuits; the one acre of agricultural land they owned did not yield enough to meet the basic needs of their large family, let alone fund an education. Ahmed followed his brother onto construction sites. Over the years, he moved from city to city in North India, learning masonry, then learning how to operate a Tremix machine. He saved money and then mobilized social networks to purchase his own Tremix machine. Today, Ahmed is a small-time contractor with his own team.[4]

Construction work changed Ahmed's life. At site, he earns thrice his family's monthly agricultural income, enabling the family to escape the extreme poverty in which they lived. Ahmed built a new home in the village and now educates his siblings. Construction work provides the dignity of work and living he was denied in his early years in school. This experience makes Ahmed a firm believer in privatization and technological skilling. Several workers like Ahmed fueled the boom in Indian construction, workers whose agrarian distress led them into construction, and who found laboring dignity through construction work. Technological advancements in construction allowed workers to upskill and secure better paying work, a move that benefited many individuals in construction.

Ahmed acknowledges and celebrates the advancements mentioned above, but also places them in perspective. He remains critical of the social structures that construction work produces. “This is hard work, but we are poor people; without hard work, we cannot survive,” he says of his working conditions. “They said we were enslaved during the British period, but I feel the shadow of enslavement exists even today.” Ahmed believes that India’s construction industry perpetuates colonial logics. “These site foremen and general managers have attained their positions because of our labor, and if we get injured, fall behind in our work, or get sick, they immediately get rid of us,” he states, highlighting the exploitation that is rife in the industry. “They say *bhagao isse* (shoo them off, also used in reference to animals) ... this hierarchy is the most disgusting thing,” Ahmed remarks.

Ahmed believes that construction lifted many people out of poverty and that technological skilling is the wave of the future. However, he is also a strong critic of the hierarchies and inequalities the industry creates, believing them to be an extension of older colonial regimes. His observations resonate in India, where many construction workers are often drawn from non-dominant castes and indigenous peoples.[5] Moreover, his insights are relevant on a global scale, as historical inequities based on ethnicity, nationalism, race, gender, and religion persist within the construction sector. These enduring inequalities continue through construction and define who designs and develops projects and who labors to build them. Architecture, through its production processes, perpetuates existing social and economic disparities, and its internal hierarchies facilitate the mistreatment, exploitation, and devaluation of labor. As Ahmed says, "I will never let my children enter this line of work, even if I have to cut my stomach [starve himself] and educate them."

Mahaab

Mahaab's fate as a mason's wife was determined for her when she was just an infant; she was engaged to her husband when she was only two months old. Mahaab shares that she comes from a family of masons, and in her community, husband-and-wife mason teams work together on construction sites. She accompanies her husband, Mohamed, acting as his assistant and is known as a *kuli* laborer (coolie). Mahaab moved to New Delhi over ten years ago when she first got married and has been working here ever since. Mahaab and Mohamed move from one construction site to another with the same contractor and always work together. Mahaab never had the opportunity to attend school; she explains that girls in her community are not educated. As an unskilled worker, Mahaab mixes cement, carries materials on her head, waters curing concrete, and sweeps up debris. She also makes tea for everyone on site. She has never been given the opportunity to build.[6]

The presence of women on construction sites, coupled with the denial of skill development opportunities for them, is pervasive in the Indian construction industry. There is a prevailing assumption that women are incapable of construction work, and many in Northern India believe that a construction site is no place for a woman (I was told that repeatedly during my fieldwork). However, many women possess not only construction skills but also contracting capabilities. They have the potential to advance in the industry. Nevertheless, most women work through their husbands.

Mahaab and her fellow women workers wake at 5:30 a.m. to bathe in the dark before cooking and cleaning for their households. Mahaab shares that she prepares one main meal for the day and another for the night. Her day begins before Mohamed's and ends after his, as she attends to their domestic needs both before and after her time on the construction site. For Mahaab and other women construction workers, their work on construction sites represents a dual form of labor: they labor to meet the needs of their families as well as build the architecture under construction. Their workdays are longer and require a diverse set of skills; however, they are denied skilling and upward mobility within the construction industry.

I often converse with Mahaab in the small, tin-walled room that she and her husband constructed as their on-site home. She shows me the bed she crafted from plywood and blocks found on site. It forms a modernist design with chunky legs. Like Mahaab, the workers fashion everyday furniture and domestic items from found materials on construction sites. Discarded plywood, steel rebar, paint cans, rope, and bamboo are commonly repurposed into functional objects. These objects demonstrate that workers not only have critiques of the industry but also design skills. Additionally, drawings of plants and animals on the walls serve as a means of self-expression and contain ecological critiques of construction. The erasure and denial of these artistic and creative abilities represent a significant loss of growth opportunities for architecture and the construction industry.[7] Construction sites are home to creative thinkers, entrepreneurs, and various skill sets, yet caste, gender, and class hierarchies continue to constrain workers. This raises the question of how to foster both creativity and equity within the structures of production.

Makeshift hard hat stand on a construction site.
(2012, Namita Vijay Dharia)

Drawing by workers on a construction site wall: mango with mango core.
(2012, Namita Vijay Dharia)

Omprakash

Omprakash, a stonemason at the Wandering Woods construction site, first caught my attention because he worked through his lunch break while others rested and slept. A quiet and diligent worker, Omprakash tells me he grew up in a small village in Uttar Pradesh. Like Ahmed, he only studied until the fifth grade; he understood that his family's economic situation would not permit him to continue his education beyond the tenth grade, leading him to believe that further study would be pointless. He describes his teenage self as a curious young man who liked to explore the world and wander around the small towns and villages in his district.

Omprakash's family did not approve of his wanderings; the family begged him to find a vocation and eventually convinced Omprakash to accompany his maternal uncle to Kashmir. There, Omprakash's uncle taught him how to work with tiles and stone. Today, twelve years later, Omprakash proudly states that his family is in a stable financial position, attributing their rise from poverty to the hard work of both himself and his father. Together, they rebuilt their tin-walled home in the village into a brick and mortar two-room one, he tells me proudly.

It was not easy for Omprakash to become a master mason and find his own work. "It is a very difficult task to come into this line [of work] and stand on your own feet," he says. Training as a worker in India's construction industry, and then surviving within it, requires a significant amount of determination, according to him. You must engage with and persuade senior masons to teach you, but also learn stealthily by looking and playing with leftover materials when no one is watching on-site. Additionally, you must convince contractors to hire you and build a social network of opportunities through other workers on-site. This demands an entrepreneurial spirit and chutzpah. Omprakash describes the level of tenacity required: "In this work, you must be like a Sarus crane," he says, referring to the well-known wetland bird of North India. "You see them standing for hours by the water, and when a fish finally comes, they quickly pounce. That is how you must be for work."

As Omprakash observes, there is a significant degree of wit and dedication inherent in the process of becoming a mason, steelworker, or carpenter. Unfortunately, this internal drive and capability are often grossly devalued by college-educated professionals on site. Many construction laborers possess a strong sense of entrepreneurship, intelligence, and a desire to escape poverty to secure better futures for their families. This means that they have the ability to expand their skill sets and develop their businesses. However, most are denied the opportunity and platform to do so, as architects and senior contractors alike believe them to be donkey workers or *gadha majdoors*, unable or not supposed to use their intellect. As a site supervisor once remarked, "the workers don't have any brains." More often than not, construction hierarchies bracket off innovation and ideation, reserving them for architects alone. This design thinking represents a lost opportunity for design and construction, as co-creating with workers can lead to new forms of collaboration, design work, and growth in architecture and design.

This still holds true, considering the diverse skill sets present on site. Omprakash describes his own skill as a stone and tile mason, "to cut stone is one of the most difficult of tasks. You must be slow and use your mind; there is a cleverness and a talent to cutting. Acquiring skills related to stone means acquiring a form of art or a high level of craftsmanship (*kala*)."

India's rich architectural history is intertwined with historic lineages of craftsmanship or *kalakars* in building construction. Like Omprakash's family, many families are part of these historic lineages of craftsmen and continue to possess skills that have been passed down through generations. However, construction work in India today often leads to deskilling and the loss of these historic skills, as architectural construction becomes increasingly monotonous and mass-produced. While several architects in India recognize historic skill sets and occasionally collaborate with craftsmen, there is much opportunity to grow collectively. Reintegrating workers' entrepreneurial and craft backgrounds into the industry allows for new design opportunities and innovative construction techniques and technologies, expanding the field through collective work.[8]

Conclusion

The dump truck winds its way down to the bottom of the pit and backs up to a cured foundation. The trapdoor at the back of the truck opens, and mud cascades down onto the footing. A cloud of dust envelops us, settling onto our skin. Jitendraji turns to me and says, "Look, Madam, all our work is dissolving in the dust (*hamari mehnat mitti mein mil rahi hai*)." He laughs. The Hindi phrase *mitti mein mil jana* is a common metaphor for hard work and time wasted due to circumstances beyond one's control. Jitendraji's tongue-in-cheek comment resonates with me as a trained, once-practicing architect and now an educator of artists and designers. He acknowledges the alienation workers feel from the architecture they create—an alienation that is not of their making. It serves as a poignant reminder that while construction labor does not literally dissolve into dust, many workers believe that they themselves do. Workers, and their labor, are effectively erased from a building after it is completed. The erasure of labor is an economic necessity to sustain and grow the construction industry.[9] There are few opportunities for workers to gain a voice and recognition within the industry.

Nevertheless, many believe there should be greater equity, support for entrepreneurship, and more value placed on the skills they possess.

The present contribution immerses us in a construction site in India's National Capital Region, highlighting the opportunities and exploitations that construction workers encounter. It urges architects and clients to engage with the inherent talents present on-site and to envision new directions for architecture through collective design and building work. To recognize design pluriverses and find ways to collectively produce and celebrate them.[10] Rather than allowing labor to proverbially dissolve into the dust, I encourage architects, developers, and contractors to reconsider the production of architecture as a collective endeavor. To explore innovative and equitable methods to build upon the skills and abilities available on-site, enabling us to expand the boundaries of design as both an aesthetic and spatial strategy, as well as a profession.

1 Malda is a district of the Indian state of West Bengal. Due to its unique location, the district is a gathering spot for workers from Northeast India, Orissa, Bihar, West Bengal, and Bangladesh.
2 All names have been changed to protect identity.
3 TFTK Production Studies, "Translating Ferro / Transforming Knowledges of Architecture, Design, and Labour for the New Field of Production Studies," https://tftk.iau.usp.br/en/

(accessed March 17, 2025); Natasha Iskander, *Does Skill Make Us Human? Migrant Workers in 21st-century Qatar and Beyond* (Princeton, NJ: Princeton University Press); Peggy Deamer, *Architecture and Labor* (London: Routledge, 2020); *The Architecture Lobby*, https://architecture-lobby.org (accessed March 17, 2025).

4 For more of Ahmed's story, see Namita Vijay Dharia, *The Industrial Ephemeral: Labor and Love in Indian Architecture and Construction* (Berkeley: University of California Press, 2022), pp. 29–33, 169.

5 In using the term "dominant caste," I am taking a cue from Suraj Yengde, "Being a Dalit," in: *Caste Matters* (New Delhi: Penguin/Viking, 2019), who disowns the upper-lower signifiers of caste and uses "non-dominant caste" and "dominant caste" instead. This use of "dominant caste" differs from M. N. Srinivas's use of the term in "The Dominant Caste in Rampura," *American Anthropologist* 61, no. 1 (1959), pp. 1–16, as, for Srinivas, "dominant caste" represents a caste that is numerically most significant in a village (such as Yadavs or Jats); https://doi.org/10.1525/aa.1959.61.1.02a00030.

6 More on Mahaab in Dharia, *The Industrial Ephemeral* (see note 4), pp. 38, 140–47, 177–78, 188, 192–94.

7 Namita Vijay Dharia, "Construction Site Pedagogies," in: Ashraf M. Salama, Harriet Harris, and Ane Gonzalez Lara, eds., *The Routledge Companion to Architectural Education in the Global South* (London: Routledge, 2022).

8 Further discussion of this can be found in Dharia, "Construction Site Pedagogies" (see note 7).

9 Dharia, *The Industrial Ephemeral* (see note 4).

10 Arturo Escobar, *Designs for the Pluriverse: Radical Interdependence, Autonomy, and the Making of Worlds* (Durham, NC: Duke University Press, 2018).

The Union, the Insurance, and the Workers: Voices from the Construction Site

Carolina Pichler and Lalie Porteret

> We can only have a more fulfilling, less passive, and more disruptive role in capitalism if we don't think of construction and labor as conceptual "others" of architecture, and, I would add, embrace its production chains.[1]—Peggy Deamer

On July 12, 2024, three construction workers perished, five were gravely injured, and six were hurt when scaffolding collapsed on a construction site in Malley, near Lausanne, Switzerland.[2] As one construction worker explained, the pace of labor on-site seems to have been an issue: "There are always so many things to do simultaneously, and very tight deadlines; it is impossible to always follow the rules. Even in Switzerland."[3] This tragedy exposed the precarity of the workforce in construction, showing that regardless of the location—here, in one of the most wealthy and privileged countries of the Northern Hemisphere—the industry pressures bodies and relies on their exploitation. With its many cranes and trucks, fences, and billboards promising highly desired spaces, Lausanne is witnessing intense construction activity, especially at the periphery. The city has 2,000 registered construction workers on 600 worksites of all types, a picture true to the sector's importance in the Swiss economy.[4] The construction industry generates around 10% of the Swiss GDP, equal to the financial sector's contribution, with nominal sales of 23.3 billion francs in 2023.[5] It employs 10% of the Swiss working population, with 330,904 workers in 2019.[6] However, the industry has suffered from a labor shortage since 2000, driven by intense activity, increased capital investment in real estate, and the accumulation of wealth in land.[7]

Value is extracted from labor costs at every turn. If architects and planners work long hours under tight deadlines to complete documents, sometimes with unpaid overtime or under fixed-fee arrangements, on-site workers experience the most direct extraction through low wages, especially among subcontracted workers. Day laborers and undocumented workers are particularly vulnerable to wage theft and unsafe conditions. The precarious reality experienced by workers stems from decisions made far from the construction site by developers, planners, and designers. Still, the industry is regulated. The trade union UNIA, the largest in the Swiss construction sector, represents workers' interests, seeking fair wages and better working conditions. It has successfully negotiated collective labor agreements for many construction workers, addressing issues like wage dumping and unsafe working conditions. SUVA (Swiss National Accident Insurance Fund) is another important actor in the construction industry as the construction sector's sole accident insurer and occupational safety authority. Operating through law, directives, employer invoices, and checklists, it provides mandatory accident insurance for workers, supervises construction sites for safety compliance, reviews company documentation, and conducts inspections. Beyond enforcement, it also functions as a service body identifying high-risk activity sectors, conducting accident investigations, providing testimony in law courts, and providing training for various stakeholders. SUVA has a hybrid status as an independent public legal entity—neither fully public nor private. Though mandated by Swiss law, it operates independently of federal administration as a nonprofit insurance company. Generally considered effective, SUVA has helped Switzerland maintain relatively low workplace accident rates, especially in construction. SUVA embodies the ongoing tension between thorough safety enforcement and the industry's desire for operational flexibility—it is often considered "a nuisance" by managerial forces. Despite these efforts, construction workers remain the most vulnerable population along the "supply chain of space production."[8]

The goal of collecting voices from the construction site is to expose the social and environmental impacts of design, to see further and question beyond labor processes in the Swiss construction industry.[9] This work examines construction sites with a focus on production pace and timing. It explores several key questions: How does the speed of work subject laborers to the construction industry's demands? What specific forms does time pressure take on construction sites? Is this pressure purely financial, or are there other dimensions to it? The construction sites we investigated present a snapshot of Switzerland's building activity, yet these observations aim to tackle issues in the construction industry at large. If architects, too, are workers producing surplus value subjected to neoliberal pressure, they should recognize their position within the construction industry's ecosystem. As scholars like Peggy Deamer and Marisa Cortright argue, all forms of labor are integrated throughout the construction production chain.[10] Neglecting the production chain erases the knowledge networks on which design relies.[11] This understanding serves as a primer to a wider dialogue on solidarity between construction industry workers.[12] The hope is to sketch possible ways of convergence in which architectural workers can enhance potential solidarity with construction workers as part of the same labor chain.

The Union: Interview with Simon Constantin (UNIA)

Collective agreements came into being largely after World War II, when there were many strikes in

Switzerland, and there was a historic compromise: "Working conditions in construction are defined between the social partners, the employers' representatives, and the unions." In other words, all companies are bound by minimum standards. In return, the workers give up striking; that is the agreement. The bosses respect their side of the labor peace; they don't close the construction site.[13] As a result, labor peace is respected in Switzerland. But that doesn't mean there aren't strikes. It's possible, it's even advisable, to go on strike to draw attention to the situation and obtain a decent social plan. Unionized and non-unionized workers, temporary workers, migrant workers, etc. are all in the same basket. If there's a negotiation with a company, it's for all employees. Our job is to try and bring everyone together. If there isn't some sort of social glue between the different categories of workers, everyone gets eaten up on their own, and no one rises up.

The major structural change over the last thirty years is speed. There was an initial phase from the late nineties to the early noughties when the increasing pace of work was accompanied by the mechanization of construction sites, with modernized machines and perfected processes. For instance, if lifting equipment is available all the time, working methods are radically different. Some processes increase the pace but aren't necessarily detrimental, like formwork panels. If you have better metals to build that go

Construction lies at the forefront of the prosperous Swiss economy.
(December 2024, Carolina Pichler, Lalie Porteret)

Workers unload one ton of concrete from a skip
(November 2024, Carolina Pichler, Lalie Porteret)

faster, all the better. Since 2010, production rates have continued to increase without major changes in the mechanization of the site; people were made to work faster. In this ultra-competitive market in which everyone is bidding on the cheapest offer, you have to make do. Sometimes, companies work at a loss. It happens regularly because it's better to leave thirty guys on payroll for six months, lose a few tens of thousands of francs, and keep them in your company to do work later. So, since 2015, the headcount has been stable, but turnover has increased.

The work pace—Monday to Friday—puts pressure on people. There's no doubt that the pressure from management spills down into construction, with planners working on tighter time frames, faster projects. It takes longer to actually start a project, with a lot of opposition, more paperwork, and more bureaucracy. Yet, there's the pressure to deliver the job on time. We don't know when we'll be able to lay the first stone, but we already know when there will be tenants or the businesses that will come to rent. So planning time has encroached on construction time, which impacts the quality of the work. In fact, the more time you have to do a good job, the more satisfied you are. Apprentices tell us it's great to take classes because they learn how to do things right. But when they arrive on-site, they know they're laying vapor barriers too fast, that won't hold, and they do it because the next job is already that afternoon.

For some people, it just doesn't make sense; they're working from 7h to 17h to get their salary at the end of the month—it's a grind. This pressure clearly has repercussions on the body. Many end up having to leave the industry after a few years—they're broken. And there hasn't been a corresponding increase in salaries either. Salaries, they're more stagnant.

Besides, the perceived overall increase in safety on worksites is tricky. The less you protect yourself, the faster you go. It's about dignity. It's a question of how much time you're given to ensure you come home safe, whole, and alive. France, for example, is far ahead of Switzerland in this respect. There's no joking with any safety standards. Whereas here in Switzerland, we're having trouble convincing SUVA that certain operations on the site are too dangerous; that they should no longer be carried out by two people, that there should be at least three; that heat waves cause deaths. When we talk about this, the bosses pass the buck to the client, the client passes to SUVA, SUVA passes to SECO. In the end, there's no solution. During the heatwave last year, we sought out the government, representatives of clients, bosses. We were able to hold discussions, but it was complicated. We often come into conflict with the employers, the employers' association, and the Société Suisse des Entrepreneurs (SSE) over issues relating to working conditions. Even though there is a shortage of construction workers. The figures are really dramatic. By 2040, there will be a shortage of one bricklayer in three, one team manager in three, and one foreman in six.[14] The demographics of the site follow a curve. There are very few young people and many old people. We peak at the age of fifty.[15] When there are quite a few apprentices on-site, and their boss doesn't have time to teach them the job, they do tasks that are uninteresting or repetitive. But then, they don't learn the job the way you'd like to learn it in an apprenticeship. Plus, there is the labor shortage, but the labor shortage for skilled labor is above all that.[16]

From the union's point of view, the worker pay classification works well with the foreman's role on-site.[17] But foremen are also put under high pressure. There are cases of burn-out among them because they have so much stress, so many demands coming from above, plus management to do on their team. They are between a rock and a hard place. What we're doing, as a union, is controlling the labor market, and keeping in view the fact that social and wage dumping are bad for everyone. It happens constantly that companies are bringing workers to Switzerland, paid ten francs an hour, then suddenly have to reduce the labor force on the site and send them back to Poland or Romania after three months.[18] These dumping practices harm everyone, without a doubt. The bad company got the job done for the same price as for a Swiss mason, and makes a profit that harms other, properly working companies. UNIA is trying to implement systematic measures to

Layers of labor entangled in the concrete slab.
(November 2024, Carolina Pichler, Lalie Porteret)

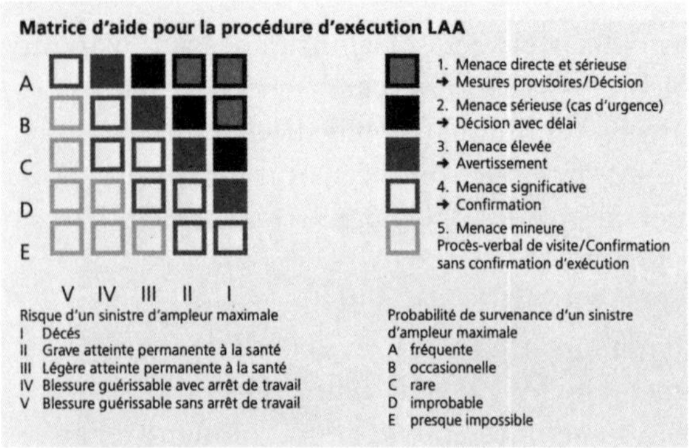

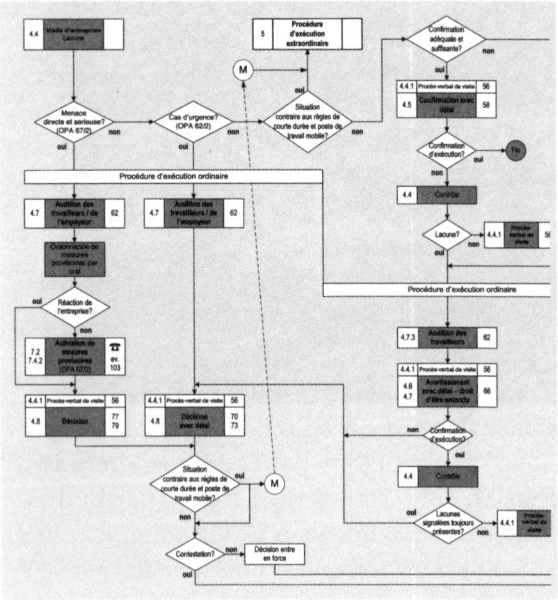

The risk matrix has two axes: the risk of loss and its severity versus probability, which is defined by accident statistics.
Bottom: Overview of the LAA enforcement procedure.

establish links between social insurance and working conditions. So as soon as there's evidence that a company isn't fulfilling its obligations, either it won't have access to public contracts, or if it subcontracts for other companies, the parent company will have to pay fines.

Working hours need to be reviewed more fundamentally. Workers do nine hours on the site, and then sometimes up two hours commute a day. The first thirty minutes of travel are unpaid. Why aren't they paid? Because there's no obligation to pay the workers in the regulations. This represents unpaid work and has the effect of increasing the length of working days. Because it's okay to steal hours from workers. It becomes a problem when you're working eleven or twelve hours a day. Repeatedly. And are you willing to put your family life on hold for that salary? Working unpaid hours is a problem across the industry.

For architects, for instance, UNIA could help, too.[19] The issue is that there is no solid employees' group or association. As a result, we have very few agreements for architects, only some at the local level, with the cantons. We do have members of the union who are architects and bring up issues from time to time. We're able to support them on an individual level. Often, it's an architect who leaves his or her office. But there's less going on for the collective struggle because we're not anchored. It's a pity because having different approaches to building construction is important. So, within that, the architect plays an important role. There's certainly thinking to be done on the question of tenders and work contracts; how you plan; how you interact with the various players; and how you organize a site. Because if you ask for big changes in policy, of course, nothing will happen. But if you ask for small, well-targeted, and well-justified changes, it's possible to change things.[20] If we had groups of architects talking about safety issues on the building site, issues of tendering, submission to tendering procedures, planning, land legislative frameworks, we could have much more impact.

The Insurance: Interview with Stephane Bettex and Michel Duinker (SUVA)

The ordinance on construction work was changed on January 1, 2022, and some things have been made more draconian. It's often true that we push for changes because we see the accident statistics. Then, there are new work methodologies. With these new methodologies, new risks can arise. There's a manual called 6030, issued by the CFST.[21] It states what the implementing bodies have to do. The assessment, made by specialists, is based on a risk matrix according to an accident's severity and probability. The higher the probability, the greater the severity, the greater the urgency, and the more drastic the measures required by the enforcement body. Then, a decision is made—a piece of paper with legal force. The company cannot object to the decision. However, it can go to court.

SUVA carries out 4,000 inspections a year. If a company has a question, we must also advise them in occupational health and safety. SUVA is funded through collecting premiums for prevention. Then, SUVA makes money, grows—the revenue, and so on. Afterward, if there were surpluses, premiums would fall the following year. For insurance premiums, the fee is a percentage of the payroll. After that, there's no fixed percentage. It depends on the class of activity and the size of the company. The larger the company, the more autonomous it is regarding security advice and support. For small- and medium-sized businesses, there is also a system based on solidarity, i.e., a premium rate that is applied to the whole of their corporation. This means that a bonus-malus system will have a greater impact on big enterprises. If, for example, a big company has fewer accidents, its premium rate will fall faster than that of the smaller companies.[22]

For foreign companies, there is a tax, a premium, or something to pay. They must comply with the same requirements as any other company. The only difference is that we can't raise its premiums. So, we're more dependent on what we see on-site—effectiveness is debatable. Generally, we look for the person who commissioned it, or we'll copy a letter to record what we've written. The fact that you have written to someone means you can pass on this letter to a cantonal inspector or copy it to SECO, who can then act against these companies. As SUVA, we can't do that. But we can stop activity on construction.

Risks have dropped by 50% since 1970.[23] The risks are separated into categories and calculated by the number of accidents per thousand workers; in 1918, it was 333 per 1000. So, about one-third of the Swiss working population insured by SUVA had an accident. Today, in the construction industry, one worker in five has an accident yearly, around 180 per 1000 workers. The people working on construction sites represent 20% of the SUVA insured and 10% of the Swiss working population, and their risk of professional accidents doubles or even triples compared to the Swiss population. They represent 40% of the SUVA accidents. It is a very dangerous industry. It's one of the worst risk categories in Switzerland.[24] We are proud to contribute to the risk of being injured or becoming ill at work having been halved over the last five years. We do our utmost to reintegrate accident victims. We have our own rehabilitation clinics in Sion and Bellikon. Almost 90% of injured people can return to working life.

The relationship between SUVA and the architect is a delicate subject. From a pure LAA point of view, the architect is responsible for its own employees, so they must provide their on-site architects with safety shoes and a helmet.[25] The primary responsibility is going to be with the employer. So, the employer says, "I'm obliged to do this." The architect says, "I don't care. I want to make a finished product like that." There can be difficulties—in this pyramid, above the normal pyramid, which has these work directions that can induce a particular dynamic."

The Workers: Voices from the Construction Site

Disclaimer

The following testimonies were collected from workers at various construction sites. All identifying information has been removed to protect participants who requested confidentiality due to fears of workplace retaliation. These accounts represent personal experiences in the construction industry and provide valuable insights into working conditions from those directly involved.

> [form worker]
>
> I work out of necessity—because I have no resources. When the pandemic came, there wasn't much work, and this is quite a stable job. We don't find work so easily because we don't know how to speak French or anything, you know what I mean?
>
> Every day we arrive an hour or half an hour earlier. We change and have coffee. We relax

afterwards. The day ends at 4:30 p.m. We work on several construction sites. When the work is finished here, we will go to another place. And the team is always changing.

You come, you do your work, and then that's it. You don't discuss much with the other teams, either, like the electricians. Everyone has their own work rhythm. There are people who work slowly, and there are people who work fast. But the work is hard. It is tough work. Physically, sometimes the body already adapts, but in principle, it is heavy. For example, a person who is not used to doing it arrives the first time and does not do well. For safety, we always use what we are asked to. For example, we put on our helmets and our work boots, and that's it, but the work we have to do is physical first. I don't know in what way one wants to say there is safety. We try to take care of ourselves, of course, because the work is dangerous. They tell us that we have to take care of ourselves, but we have to do the work. Nothing happens if you are sick and miss two days of work. But if you miss more than two days, you must go to the doctor, who gives you a leave of absence or brings a paper or something.

We have a manager who tells us what to do. The bosses are very difficult; we don't have relationships with them.

[electrician]

On construction sites, planning is a disaster. The deadlines are too short, and there is a cruel lack of employees because not enough are trained. On the other hand, here on the site, you come in at 7 a.m. and leave at 4 p.m. It is clear. And from time to time, you have to do some overtime.

We are [engaged] per element. That means we are engaged to do this wall, engaged to do this other wall, engaged to do this slab, but … next Tuesday, we will have the final decision on whether we stay until the end or not.

If we had time, imagine! On a building site, we have two and a half days to pipe the slab before they come to put on the second layer. We'd have things lined up, perfectly lined up. And then, in fact, they [other workers] can walk in places where they don't need to walk on a tube. Here, given that we have one day to pipe a slab and that we'd have to take two, inevitably, there are tubes in every direction.

[mason]

You have to give it time because, at some point, we will pay for it.… The concrete isn't dry; they [the DT: Directeur de Travaux, or construction site manager] want the same rate as for precast. It's not possible.

1 Peggy Deamer, *Architecture and Labor* (New York: Routledge, 2020), https://doi .org/10.4324/9780429325182 (accessed March 28, 2025).
2 État de Vaud, 'Accident mortel sur un chantier à Prilly – dernier point de situation', État de Vaud, July 16, 2024, https://www.vd.ch /actualites/actualite/news/i-accident-mortel -sur-un-chantier-a-prilly-dernier-point-de -situation (accessed April 15, 2025).
3 Margaux Habert, "Echafaudage à Malley: 'Il aurait pu y avoir plus de morts,'" *Watson*, July 15, 2024, https://www.watson.ch/fr/!239974251 (accessed April 15, 2025).
4 Simon Constantin, UNIA, interview with the authors, November 25, 2024.
5 Martin Maniera, "Chiffre d'affaires 2023," *Société Suisse des Entrepreneurs*, February 28, 2024, https://baumeister.swiss/fr/apres-une -bonne-annee-2023-2024-sannonce-decisive -pour-la-construction-de-logements-et -dinfrastructures/#:~:text=L'activit%C3%A9% 20de%20construction%20a,effectif%20de%20 0%2C9%25 (accessed April 15, 2025).
6 Luiza Maria Maniera, "Il va de l'avant depuis 125 ans: les évolutions du secteur de la construction," *Société Suisse des Entrepreneurs*, April 19, 2022, https://baumeister.swiss/fr /il-va-de-lavant-depuis-125-ans-les-evolutions -du-secteur-de-la-construction/ (accessed April 15, 2025).
7 Manuel Buchmann et al., *Étude sur l'évolution à long terme de l'activité économique et de la maind'œuvre qualifiée dans le secteur principal de la construction* (Bâle: Demografik, 2022), available at *Société Suisse des Entrepreneurs*, https://baumeister.swiss/sbv-veroeffentlicht

-studie-zum-fachkraeftemangel-im-bauhauptgewerbe/ (accessed April 15, 2025).

8 See Charlotte Malterre-Barthes, "Architecture of Extraction," in: Justinien Tribillion et al., eds., *Visible Upon Breakdown: Exploring the Cultural, Political, and Spatial Nature of Infrastructure* (Berlin: Spector 2024).

9 Charlotte Malterre-Barthes, ed., *On Architecture and Greenwashing*, The Political Economy of Space, Vol. 1 (Berlin: Hatje Cantz, 2024).

10 See Peggy Deamer, *Architecture and Labor* (New York: Routledge, 2020), https://doi.org/10.4324/9780429325182; Marisa Cortright, *"Can This Be? Surely This Cannot Be?": Architectural Workers Organizing in Europe* (Prague: VI PER Gallery, 2021), p. 7.

11 Namita Vijay Dharia, *The Industrial Ephemeral: Labor and Love in Indian Architecture and Construction* (Berkeley: University of California Press, 2022), p. 16.

12 Swarnabh Ghosh, "Toward a Critique of Labor in Construction," in *Non-Extractive Architecture: On Designing without Depletion*, Vol. 1 (London: Sternberg Press, 2021), p. 160.

13 [Business owners and managers do not often enter into management strikes.—Ed.]

14 Buchmann et al., *Étude* (see note 6).

15 Retirement age in Switzerland is 64 (women), 65 (men). In 2024, UNIA, along with other unions, achieved early retirement for bricklayers at the age of 60. This has set a precedent for early retirement in other trades.

16 Buchmann et al., *Étude* (see note 6).

17 SM, A, B, C, Q.

18 [Switzerland does not have a federally mandated minimum wage. Minimum wages are set by cantons and through collective labor agreements (CLAs) for specific industries. Geneva, Neuchâtel, Jura, Ticino, and Basel-Stadt have cantonal minimum wages. A government report found severe and rampant violations of Swiss wage levels, working

conditions, and wage dumping when employing foreign workers. Keystone-SDA, "One in Five Checks Reveals Violations of Swiss Labour Regulations," *SWI*, June 10, 2024, https://www.swissinfo.ch/eng/workplace-switzerland/one-in-five-checks-reveals-violations-of-swiss-labour-regulations/80259032 (accessed April 15, 2025).—Ed.]

19 In Geneva, there's a movement to have a specialized union to get a CCT (Convention Collective de Travail, a collective trade agreement) for fixed working hours.

20 For instance, UNIA introduced two interventions in parliament aimed at postponing deadlines when construction work is interrupted due to adverse weather conditions. According to the Swiss Engineers and Architects (SIA) norm 118 Contract 4, which defines contractual obligations, project deadlines must be extended if delays occur through no fault of the contractor. However, SIA standards are not legally mandatory—if a client chooses to exclude SIA 118 from the contract, the legal protections contractors assume to be in place are null and void. To address this issue, UNIA has called on parliament to make this provision compulsory. Such policy changes can be successful if properly strategized.

21 [The Swiss Federal Commission for Occupational Health and Safety (CSFT) coordinates and oversees occupational health and safety measures nationwide. It collaborates with the Swiss National Accident Insurance Fund (SUVA)—established under the 1918 Federal Accident Insurance Act (AIA)—to implement and enforce the 1984 Accident Insurance Act (LAA) and its sub-ordinances (OPA, OTConst, Crane Ordinance) in high-risk occupational sectors. The LAA, OPA, and OTConst are laws designed for businesses and employers to guarantee the health and safety of their employees.—Ed.]

22 A bonus rate is applied to small- and medium-sized businesses, affecting the entire entity, which may see its rate increase or decrease accordingly. According to SUVA, considering the threshold, the impact of an individual company is relatively limited.

23 SUVA, "Notre modèle d'affaires: mieux qu'une assurance," *Suva*, https://www.suva.ch/fr-ch/autoportrait/la-suva/suva-modele-daffaires (accessed April 15, 2025).

24 SUVA, "Séries chronologiques des accidents par classe – 41A Secteur principal de la construction," *Statistik der Unfallversicherung* UVG, https://unfallstatistik.ch/f/neuza/Suva_Kl_f/WirtKl_BUV_41A.pdf (accessed April 15, 2025).

25 Loi fédérale sur l'assurance-accidents (LAA) is the federal legal framework that renders mandatory accident insurance for employees working in Switzerland, under which the SUVA manages the most risky professional sectors.

Architecture, Politics, and Self-management: *Mutirão* as a Transformative Practice

Usina-CTAH with Pedro Fiori Arantes[1]

In Brazil, *mutirão* is a self-managed construction process in which future residents collectively build their own housing with architects' technical support, using public funds. It stands as a place of invention for autonomist practices and the strengthening of popular organizations, with visible repercussions—starting with the quality of built space, much different from the conventional housing complexes or the auto-construction done by other residents in the periphery of cities.[2]

In the nineteen-seventies, university students and the "Brazilian people" resumed working together in the struggle for housing, a practice abruptly interrupted by the 1964 military coup.[3] It was mostly architects, students, and social workers who went to the periphery and favelas to engage in daily activism with these communities and emerging movements.

"Self-management" became an alternative to other forms of organization, always accompanied by disputes for distributing public funds, occupation of land, and manifestations of all sorts. Demands for public policy accompanied the refusal of top-down state implementation. This created a central paradox: seeking government resources while maintaining independence from state control.

The transforming autonomist practices of popular management were put to the test in the early nineteen-eighties and -nineties during the "re-democratization" of the country, characterized by the external debt crisis and, consequently, public spending cuts. New public policies were defined during a moment of democratic opening associated with the developmentalism crisis and the direct intervention of its multilateral agencies, such as the International Monetary Fund, the United Nations Organization, and the World Bank. They unexpectedly found "virtues" in the capacities of the so-called poor to be responsible for their own social reproduction. Simultaneously, the Workers' Party (Partido dos Trabalhadores, PT) achieved its first electoral victories, which spurred an unexpected state alliance with social movements. For São Paulo specifically, it resulted in the democratic creation of post-dictatorship public policies that included housing and the self-managed *mutirões* under Luiza Erundina's administration (1989–92). From this tension a question emerged: Is *mutirão* genuine grassroots empowerment or another neoliberal approach that shifts responsibility to the poor?

Co-opted Language

Social movements' mobilization outside the state, but with public resources, establishes an important space to strengthen popular struggles and practices and construct an alternative counter-power.

The semantic confusion between "self-help" and "self-management" with which we are confronted today originates in the nineteen-seventies. The World Bank had started promoting "self-help" approaches to social programs that superficially resembled self-management. But for populations excluded from the formal economy, these programs presented unpaid beneficiary labor as a "feasible and responsible practice" in the face of large-scale government interventions with budget deficits of developing countries.

Giving "power to the users" and beneficiaries of public policies while cutting social program spending became a World Bank motto, glossing over the slogans of the British anarchist architect John Turner.[4] In the turbulent seventies, authoritarian and modernizing states became the target of both liberal and left-wing criticism, while the World Bank's agendas and documents co-opted the left's ideas and slogans—a tactic that Vera Telles characterizes as "semantic slippage," in which the same words come to mean other things. This occurred in the construction of the solidary-managerial lexicon of the neoliberal years. Not only does the World Bank capture the left's words, but the left also reproduces the former's managerial and "best practices" discourse, creating a "single language" in which it is no longer possible to distinguish who is using it. This linguistic co-optation obscures crucial differences in ideology and practice.

Again, in the nineteen-nineties, the World Bank pushed self-help policies to governments, now adorned with the rhetoric of "solidarity," yet this time with the support of non-governmental organizations. According to Pierre Bourdieu, this rhetoric "allows one to 'accuse the victim,' the only one responsible for his misfortune, and preach 'self-help.'"[5]

An intense argument between the classes occurs, in which one cannot distinguish who is who because everyone is saying the same thing.[6] However, upon closer analysis of practices, one recognizes in popular movements' actions initiatives that cannot be discursively co-opted: the occupation of land and public agencies, the sense of confrontation, clashes with the holders of economic and political power, criticism of the development model, independent structures of activists' training, slogans, and narratives that spell out a different story. In short, everything related to constructing a "popular power" with some autonomy and anti-capitalist aspirations.

Unlike neoliberal policies, which present preconceived solutions for a focalized and passive demand, the *mutirões* are part of a long process of the popular movement's struggle to fulfill the basic need for shelter, strengthen its organizations, and increase activists' awareness. In this struggle, public funds, as an accumulation of socially produced wealth, are under dispute in all their significance.

It is important to remember that the *mutirões* were—and still are—fundamentally a political movement with coordinated, militant organization. In the early nineteen-eighties, social movements seized technical and organizational autonomy from the state while establishing higher quality standards for construction processes and built environments. This challenged the prevailing authoritarian, mercantile public housing approach controlled by Brazil's powerful construction companies (the so-called "republic of contractors"). These advances redefined how organized communities engaged with the state—particularly in project management—and emerged from widespread popular mobilization for urban reform and broader societal transformation. This collective approach stood in stark contrast to the individualized solutions prevalent in growing cities, where residents relied on personal savings to fund technically inadequate, self-built housing in irregular settlements.

Self-management and *Mutirão*: Paradoxes of a Future Form Lived Presently

The self-managed *mutirão* is a workers' association that produces housing for direct use rather than market exchange—a *sui generis* good. While what is produced is an object—a home—that crystalizes work/labor and possesses use value (with potential exchange value), it has not been planned for sale and capital accumulation.

Unlike cooperatives that must operate within market logic, the *mutirão*'s self-management directly engages with the state, requiring public funds while explicitly contesting how social wealth is distributed. This difference distinguishes the *mutirão* from conventional contractors—subjected to wage relationships—and from a construction cooperative—subjected to market competition—a distinction that requires deeper analysis to understand its transformative potential.

Yet, like the cooperative, the *mutirão* is a paradoxical space of freedom, though with different foundations. This is most evident in the organization of ephemeral work: once housing construction concludes, residents return to their dependent relationship with the labor market, with no structural change in how they must sell their labor power to survive. In this sense, the *mutirão* differs fundamentally from cooperatives, which provide a sustained alternative to wage labor. However, comparing these distinct production modes (as experienced, for example, by the Landless Workers' Movement [Movimento dos Trabalhadores sem Terra, or MST], which engages in both) helps illuminate the experimental value of the *mutirão* approach.[7] Landless people joined the MST with a precise goal: securing a dwelling, a fundamental necessity for survival. The movement presents *mutirão* as the preferred approach for housing production. The starting point is one of rupture: marches, land occupations, and encampments—followed by a phase of integration, in which the movement demands inclusion in public policies and access to state funding for construction. These resources remain limited and subject to state control—it can veto the movement's decisions about design and technology or effectively halt construction by withholding funds.

Integration into public policy, however, creates strategic dilemmas for the movement: it risks co-optation, pragmatism, or confrontation—the latter potentially jeopardizing access to resources. Without comprehensive political education that helps members critically analyze their daily struggles, the movement may lose its balance between resistance and integration. Yet, without engaging with state resources, participants are forced back into individual self-construction, personal savings, and market-based solutions.

Mutirão União da Juta was completed in 1997 with Usina, which was responsible for the project and site management. It was financed by the Urban Housing Development Company and was organized by Associação União da UTA, affiliated to MST Leste 1. Located in the São Mateus neighborhood of São Paulo, the project comprises 160 units, and its innovation was in the use of metal stair towers erected after the foundations were laid. (2024, Usina-CTAH)

The stair towers served a double function, allowing the safe transport of people and materials as well as providing visibility to the building. The housing units were erected around the stairs, which eliminated construction beams and pillars (often complex and costly due to the formwork and reinforcement required). Then, housing units were made in load-bearing ceramic blocks, thereby avoiding the costs and risk of accidents associated with plastering and facade scaffolding. In this way, the work was radically simplified and rationalized. (2007, Usina-CTAH)

Located in the Cidade Tiradentes neighborhood of São Paulo, Mutirão Paulo Freire's 100 "free plan" apartment units were made possible by the metal structure and non-load-bearing walls. Three "bridge" structures, each composed of three apartments, were built to link the five- and seven-story buildings. These suspended apartments eliminated the need for an entirely new building and left space for a communal plaza. (2024, Usina-CTAH)

The technical advisory agency that supports the movement's action, in turn, has an extremely delicate role of preserving technical knowledge that can hardly be socialized. In economist Michael Albert's view, self-management means that each agent must participate in decision-making in the same proportion in which they are affected by its consequences.[8] In this sense, specialized knowledge should be disseminated to the maximum so that each agent involved can draw their own conclusion. Even though the technical advisory agency provided by architects always seeks to collectivize its knowledge, there are clear limits—for example, the majority of activists lack the basic training that would enable them to handle elementary tools of knowledge (mathematics, physics, geometry, logic, writing, etc.).

A technical premise of the *mutirão,* enabled by its relative autonomy, is the exploration of innovative means of production, designs, and resultant building forms. However, this experimental approach primarily stems from the technical advisor's knowledge, which is not fully shared by all those involved in the *mutirão*. Therefore, a *mutirão* is an alliance between different actors with various origins: university-educated architects, technicians, and organized community members. This places architects and technical advisors in a complex position. While they strive for knowledge-sharing and dialogue with community members practicing the *mutirão*'s self-management, they inevitably retain concentrated technical expertise—and consequently, significant decision-making influence—particularly during the design and construction phases. Minimizing the role of designers and technical agents, though desirable, is not yet possible. Meanwhile, mainstream society, stripped of autonomous creativity and dominated by commodity fetishism, habitually defers to market-driven solutions, accepting consumer "power of choice" as natural and inevitable. This mindset is exemplified by the propaganda of the former mayor of São Paulo, Paulo Maluf, who claimed that "[t]he dream of every favela dweller is the Cingapura"[9]—so, why do it differently?

Since technical knowledge has not yet fully merged with popular movements (a goal the movement actively pursues), open and critical—but not antagonistic—dialogue between these allies remains essential. For this purpose, the technical advisory agencies must also be self-managed collectives. Usina, the collective and technical advisory agency in which we participate, is a radically horizontal group: All administrative, design, and political decisions are made collectively in meetings where everyone has an equal voice and vote. Functions rotate to alternate who publicly represents the entity, and equal hourly wages are maintained (everyone receives the same hourly rate), regardless of experience or responsibility. This does not exempt us from other contradictions, like dealing with a hybrid role of paid professionalism and activism. However, this structure establishes a position of equality with the associations and movements with which Usina works—it establishes the equality necessary for authentic dialogue with movements about self-management because we practice what we advocate.

The *mutirão*—the technical advisory agency, or the cooperative's self-management—consists in its approaches, verifications, and tests of what it could become. However, this exists alongside harsh market realities. For instance, conventional contractors with poor labor practices are hired to supplement the self-managed workforce to accelerate construction progress. This contradiction is a shadow hovering over the entire experience—one that the movement and its technical advisors typically choose to ignore.

What is the strange novelty of the *mutirão*? It is not producing goods with the immediate purpose of capital exchange and valorization, which imbues it with a different *quality*. This distinction, in combination with the relative horizontality of work on the construction site and the collectivization of decisions, the use of social wealth accumulated in the public funds, and a differentiated technical perspective, are critical points that enable a certain rupture with the logic of the capitalist system. Certainly, the *mutirão* alone does not bring the possibility of transforming the system. However, the relations of production demonstrated and experimented with in the *mutirão* can constitute alternatives to the capitalist mode of production. Thus, the *mutirão* raises important topics of discussion concerning the political economy of space.

The predominance of use over exchange is not a secondary theme. It indicates that the production of space could exist beyond capitalist forms of production, in which the use value and the preservation of physical and work know-how prevail in design and execution decisions. In this way, production would be guided by the quality of materials and spaces (as a final product) and the adequacy of techniques to the requirements of the work (as production process). The capitalist mentality of increasing productivity and labor exploitation while reducing product quality and lifespan would cease to dominate production. The disconnect between form and content would be questioned: How different are the spaces produced with a new mode of production? The techniques adopted cannot continue to be the same, or at least not for the same reasons. The adequacy of the technique to the work and the final product takes on another role in production. This does not mean a regression—the more advanced techniques can be used insofar as they follow the definitions provided by *mutirão* self-management.

When use prevails, experimentation has a greater chance to develop. It should be measured by collective decisions and adequate techniques, but it has broader limiting parameters related to the act of production for exchange. These parameters are highly justified socially and politically, not economically. The self-managed-*mutirão*-form raises yet another important question: How does the connection between form and content enable an ethical reflection on technique? The current technological apparatus does not deny its authoritarian character, "the peculiar noise of the factory muffles the thoughts."[10] In self-management, production techniques must be different, re-humanizing the human instead of transforming it into an automaton.

According to the architect Sérgio Ferro, unlike the industrial rhythm of industries, architectural production—which is close to the workers' knowledge, still semi-artisanal, still a manufacturing process—encourages personal and collective creativity. This characteristic would enable it to be the most radical of arts, allowing experimentation by free producers in dialogue.[11] The architectural field keeps these and other possibilities as a work that is unique, territorial, and tectonic, to be used, lived, and transformed, that responds to physical and spiritual needs.

Thus, the social dimension of work emerges from all the dimensions of sociability. The issue of gender is noteworthy, and it appears in practice when women position themselves as equals. This abrupt change

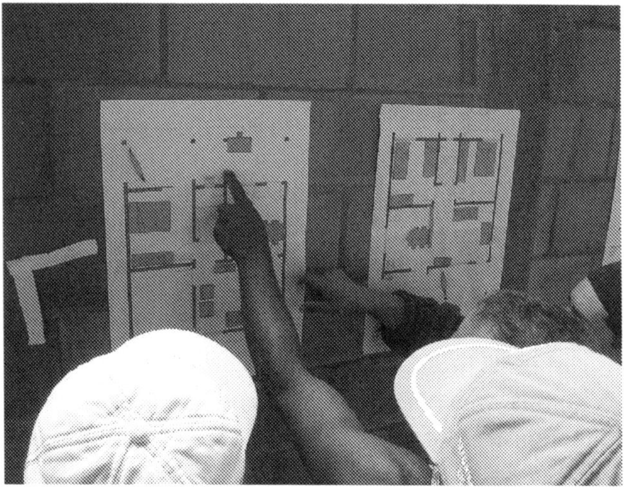

Mutirão Comuna da Terra Dom Tomas Balduíno (61 housing units in an agrarian reform settlement in the municipality of Franco Da Rocha, metropolitan region of São Paulo) was initiated by a university extension group from the Universidade de São Paulo (USP) and was funded by two public funds, National Institute of Colonization and Agrarian Reform and Caixa Econômica Federal. The MST contracted Usina to complete the project, secure financing approval, and execute the work with the settlement members. After discussion, six housing typologies of ceramic blocks of about 70 m^2 were approved. The project used a decentralized workflow across 61 scattered plots. (2007, Usina-CTAH)

in social relations raises profound questions that permeate people's daily lives, from work to marriage, challenging traditional gender roles everywhere. Civil construction is one of the most violent spaces of production, presenting the highest rates of accidents and deaths; hence, workplace safety, accident prevention, and the reduction of fatigue are also important issues to be tackled. In the *mutirão*, the survival and well-being of fellow participants become an actual goal (and not merely to avoid fines and labor lawsuits, as contractors do) simply because the aim is to preserve everyone until the end of the process—otherwise, the struggle would be senseless.

The *mutirão* brings about changes in various scales. In sociability, in the political relationship between individuals, in their relationship with society, in the relations of production, and in the type of product created. This is not about social revolution per se. The question we must ask is whether or not these changes accumulate in relevant *practices* for the constitution of popular power, or if they create a field of possibilities for organization and sociability that are impossible in the capitalist system and, for that matter, form a counterweight to it.

Moving from theory to practical application, the self-managed *mutirão* is not a model of universal housing policy and has never been presented as such. It is a space of resistance and organization and a visualization of a new type of practice. No

Vaulted roof construction using metal formwork sized on the reach of a mason's arm, which doubled as scaffolding. The shell was disassembled into smaller parts, transportable by workers between houses. Seven vaulted houses were completed within a few months. (2024, Usina-CTAH)

popular power can sustain itself solely on marches, occupations, conventions, programs, and theories. Its achievements must happen in daily life in response to basic needs. This has been known for some time, here in Latin America, at least since Sierra Maestra, and in Brazilian Ecclesiastical Base Communities (Comunidades Eclesiais de Base).[12] Radical practice happens only if intellectuals are, in fact, on the side of the people, seeking collective solutions, from the most prosaic things (shelter) to the highest spiritual issues (discussions on art, socialism, etc.). Such experiences would be multiplied, in fact, only in the revolutionary transition.

1 Published in *Revista Urbania* 3 (2007). Usina—Centro de Trabalhos para o Ambiente Habitado (Usina-CTAH) is an interdisciplinary technical advisory agency (*assessoria técnica*) that provides support to movements of landless people in their struggle for housing (housing, community centers, schools, squares, etc.). See author biographies, p. 109.

2 *Mutirão* (plural *mutirões*) is a Brazilian Portuguese word for self-building, a combination of "mutual help" and "task force." It originally comes from Tupí-Guaraní, a family of Brazilian indigenous languages as defined by Daniela Sandler in "Social-Interest Architecture in Brazil: The Seed of Something New," in Duanfang Lu, ed., *The Routledge Companion to Contemporary Architectural History* (New York: Routledge, 2021). [In the Brazilian context, "periphery" (periferia) is more than a geographic location; it designates socio-spatially marginalized areas characterized by distance from urban centers, socioeconomic vulnerability,

self-built housing, irregular land occupation, and limited infrastructure.—Ed.]

3 [The term "o povo brasileiro"—the Brazilian people—goes beyond the definition of the population living in Brazil. Progressive groups invoke it to highlight the struggles of marginalized communities and to advocate for more inclusive policies.—Ed.]

4 On the World Bank's agendas and Turner's ambiguous role, see Mike Davis, "As ilusões do construa-você-mesmo," in *Planeta Favela* (São Paulo: Boitempo, 2006); and Pedro Arantes, "O ajuste urbano: as políticas do Banco Mundial e do BID para as cidades latino-americanas," (master's thesis, FAU-USP, São Paulo, 2004).

5 Pierre Bourdieu, *Contrafogos. Táticas para enfrentar a invasão neoliberal* (Rio de Janeiro: Zahar, 1998), pp. 15–16.

6 Paulo Arantes, "Esquerda e direita no espelho das ONGs," in *Zero à Esquerda* (São Paulo: Conrad, 2004). In a seminar recently organized by Caixa Econômica Federal (CEF) and Financiadora de Estudos e Projetos (FINEP) to discuss an intriguing "Social Technologies Network," in which Usina participated, an eminent university professor argued that when a middle-class individual signs a contract for a project, hires labor, obtains financing, and manages a construction site, he/she becomes a "self-management agent."

7 In an urban environment, the dwelling can be understood as "the place of workforce reproduction," as distinct from the place of production. The *mutirões* experiment with the construction site as a "place of reproduction" only while construction works are underway. When the dwellings are ready, they are only occasionally used as a locus of production (when dwellers, as a survival strategy, set up beauty salons, auto-mechanic shops, and commerce in their homes). Whereas, given the characteristics of rural patterns of existence, agrarian reform

settlements promote the superposition of the place of production and workforce reproduction.

8 Michael Albert, "Buscando a autogestão," in *Autogestão Hoje: Teorias e Práticas Contemporâneas* (São Paulo: Faísca Publicações Libertárias, 2004).

9 [Cingapura (Portuguese for Singapore), was a program inspired by the Asian city's mass housing model—the Housing and Development Board (HDB), run by the city of São Paulo in the nineties during Mayor Paulo Maluf's administration, aiming to build housing complexes for favela dwellers.—Ed.]

10 Murray Bookchin, "Autogestão e tecnologias alternativas," in *Autogestão Hoje: Teorias e Práticas Contemporâneas* (São Paulo: Faísca Publicações Libertárias, 2004).

11 Sérgio Ferro, *Arquitetura e trabalho livre* (São Paulo: CosacNaify, 2006).

12 Fidel Castro led the Cuban Revolution from the Sierra Maestra mountain range in Cuba.

Contributors

Pedro Fiori Arantes

Pedro Fiori Arantes is an architect, urban planner, and professor of Art History at the School of Philosophy, Languages, and Human Sciences of the Federal University of São Paulo. He has been a member of the Usina collective since 1999, providing technical assistance to grassroots social movements. He has published numerous articles, chapters, and books on housing, the right to the city, culture and politics, and architectural criticism. He is the author of *The Rent of Form: Architecture and Labor in the Digital Age* (University of Minnesota Press, 2019). He is the editor of the works of Sérgio Ferro in Brazil, an author who radically transformed architectural criticism by framing it from the perspective of architecture from below, through the lens of labor in construction work.

Usina-CTAH

Usina — Centro de Trabalhos para o Ambiente Habitado is a Brazil-based interdisciplinary technical advisory agency (*assessoria técnica*) that provides support to movements of landless people in their struggle for housing but also community centers, daycare centers, schools, public squares, etc. Founded in 1991, Usina has worked on projects with worker participation, in which workers plan, design, and build their own homes, mainly in the states of São Paulo, Minas Gerais, and Paraná. Usina also worked on developing urban plans, the urbanization of favelas, and the formation and organization of work cooperatives, articulating alternatives to the commercial and authorial production of space, architecture, and urbanism. Usina is also an advocate of urban and agrarian reforms.

Marisa Cortright

Marisa Cortright researched the archive of Swedish architect and designer Susanne Wasson Tucker at ArkDes in Stockholm in 2023–24. As guest editor of the *Avery Review* in 2023, she conducted a project on architectural workers organizing against injustice and commissioned an essay from the Alternative Building Industry Collective. In 2021, she published a book of essays, *"Can This Be? Surely This Cannot Be?" Architectural Workers Organizing in Europe* with VI PER Gallery, and in 2019, she published the article "Death to the Calling: A Job in Architecture is Still a Job" in *Failed Architecture*. She holds architectural and urban history degrees from the Bartlett School of Architecture and Barnard College.

Namita Vijay Dharia

Namita Vijay Dharia is an associate professor of Anthropology and Political Economy at the

Rhode Island School of Design. She has a PhD in Anthropology from Harvard University and a MArch in architecture from Cornell University. She is the author of the *Industrial Ephemeral: Labor and Love in Indian Architecture and Construction*, a monograph published with the University of California Press in its Atelier series. She works across the themes of materiality and aesthetic studies, political ecology, labor studies, and planning and development politics. Dharia has practiced and taught architecture in India and the United States, worked as an architectural journalist, and collaborated on design research projects. She is working on her second book-length project, which studies the urban infrastructures of sleep in spatial, environmental, and labor relations in Mumbai, India, focusing on the significance of urban and planetary un/rest.

Charlotte Malterre-Barthes

Charlotte Malterre-Barthes is an architect, urban designer, and Assistant Professor at the Swiss Federal Institute of Technology (EPFL), where she leads the RIOT laboratory. Malterre-Barthes investigates contemporary urbanization, material extraction, climate emergency, and ecological/social justice. While Assistant Professor at the Harvard Graduate School of Design, she initiated the call for *A Moratorium on New Construction*, interrogating current development protocols (Sternberg/MIT Press, 2025). She holds a PhD from ETH Zurich on the political economy of commodities in the built environment and is the coauthor of several prize-winning books, including *Migrant Marseille* and *Housing Cairo*. She cofounded the Parity Front and the Parity Group (Meret Oppenheim Prize 2023), militant grassroots collectives laboring toward equity in architecture.

(non-)Swiss Architects

(non-)Swiss Architects is a collective of workers in architecture, landscape architecture, urban design and planning in private practices and education based in Zurich that advocates for the improvement of working conditions in Switzerland, started in 2021 as a reaction to the problematic everyday dynamics of design firms and from the need to share personal experiences. Overwork, underpay, and unequal treatment of workers of different backgrounds are among the widespread issues (non-)Swiss Architects investigate and bring to light through research and communication. Their work is guided by the desire to safeguard and expand workers' rights for Swiss and non-Swiss persons alike in every canton, with no distinctions based on gender and background. (non-)Swiss architects believe that an ethically designed and constructed environment can only be produced by workers with fair working conditions. By connecting and collaborating with other advocacy groups, (non-)Swiss Architect actively contributes to a solidarity network in Switzerland and beyond.

Carolina Pichler

Carolina Pichler is a master's student in architecture at EPFL with a bachelor's degree from EPFL. Active in university politics, she contributes to the associations TNT (Transition vers une Nouvelle Culture du Travail), which addresses working conditions, and the Drag Lab, which promotes diversity in architecture education. Since 2024, she has been a student assistant at the RIOT laboratory. Through internships, rammed earth construction, and studio projects, Carolina explores decarbonization, material extraction, and labor value in design practices. Her diploma work (MArch 2025) with Lalie Porteret, supervised by the RIOT laboratory, critically examines labor processes on Swiss construction sites and advocates for centering labor within architectural practice.

Lalie Porteret

Lalie Porteret is a master's student in architecture at EPFL with a bachelor's degree from the National School of Architecture in Strasbourg (ENSAS). Active in university politics, she contributes to associations TNT (Transition vers une Nouvelle Culture du Travail), which addresses working conditions, and the Drag Lab, which promotes diversity in architecture education. She is a student assistant at ALICE laboratory for first-year project teaching. Her diploma work (MArch 2025) with

Carolina Pichler, supervised by the RIOT laboratory, critically examines labor processes on Swiss construction sites and advocates for centering labor within architectural practice. Lalie investigates labor and material extraction in architectural practices through on site internships, rammed earth and cob construction or academic projects.

RIOT (Research and Innovation On Territory)

The RIOT laboratory comprises a group of affiliated individuals engaged in pedagogy, research, and action within the Institute of Architecture (ENAC) at the Swiss Federal Institute of Technology (EPFL), led by Charlotte Malterre-Barthes with Elif Erez-Henderson, Summer Islam, Antoine Iweins, Kathlyn Kao, Nagy Makhlouf, Nathalie Marj, and Saira Mohamed. Believing that the construction sector and design disciplines must pivot and wholeheartedly engage in the current social and climatic urgencies by rewiring themselves to face and repair existing harm, RIOT utilizes tactics and strategies to decarbonize, decolonize, and depatriarchalize space production—by design.

Acknowledgments

Thanks to Kathlyn Kao for her managerial and editorial work in this publication, Wulf Böer, Shant Chaorian, Tom Emerson, Olaf Grawert, Summer Islam, Khensani Jurczok-de Klerk, Nikolaos Magouliotis, Mathilde Marendaz, Lucía Jalón Oyarzun, Dubravka Sekulić, Leonard Streich, Cindy Yiin, and Noémie Zurbriggen for joining our reviews for the "Fix the Office" Design Studio (spring 2024) at EPFL, as well as the students who took this class: Malak Abdelhady, Albert Assy, Francesco Alberto, Lalie Bays, Pauline Ehrhardt, Anna Hausel, Laszlo Hofmann, Melanny Jacome, Marie Jelk, Dora Joppien, Hanna Lindenberg-Kappmeyer, François Mégret, Nanda Nugraha, Eva Oustric, Gabriel Ogbonna, Ecenaz Ozkorkut, Auguste Pachoud, Débora Pereira, Julia Petrachenko, ZL Louis Queloz, Kemmett Saunders-Nazareth, Melina Schechinger, Jacob Schlüssel, Phileas Schulhof, Prudence Vanpoulle, Juliette Vincent.

Thanks to the RIOT team past and present: Paulina Ornella Beron, Laure Melati Dekoninck, Elif Erez-Henderson, Summer Islam, Antoine Iweins, Marie-Christine Lehmann, Kathlyn Kao, Nagy Makhlouf, Nathalie Marj, Saira Mohamed, Eva Oustric, Tamara Pelège, Carolina Pichler.

Thank you to the students of the studio "Political Spaces" at TU Berlin (2018–19), Jakob Adler, Davide Broggio, Sofia Vila Clavell, Laura Dandrada de Almeida, Natalya Dikhanov, Huichao Ding, Jieqiong Gao, Guilherme Gaspar, Francesco Grillo,Elisabeth Haentjes, Paul Harries, Sacha Jonckers, Maximilian Kessler, Katharina Kocol, Lya Kröger, Inka Marie Kuik, Valentina Nadwornicek, Katarzyna Obarzanowska, Zeynep Sena Oktar, Monika Pawlak, Felix Reiter, Anatol Rettberg, Mick Riesenberg, Mascha Ritter, Clara Salaün, Cecilia Santamaría, Felix Schöllhorn, Anna-Maria Tiedemann, Camille Valette, Lisa Sophie Woebcken (2018); Daniel Baše, Cansu Bulduk, Olivia Daw, Yara Dessoky, Sarah Liz Dietz, Sarah Gretsch, James Heusser-Kowoll, Jennifer Jiang, Sinali Lal d'Aram de Valada, Liv Lees, Ioanna Nicolaou, Mathilde Pagneux, Daniel Platon,Tayfun Saman, Ludwig Thanhäuser (2019), and the students of the workshop "Construction as Site" at Politecnico di Milano (2025): Irene Bacchin, Alice Bilzi, Luna Bukumirovic, Mandi Chen, Anna Chiara Ciapetti, Elisa Leutner, Filippo Lucia, Riccardo Marvulli, Ilaria Masciarelli, Vittoria Pagliari, Alessandro Maria Vignali, Xiaolin Yan, Giorgia Zamperetti, and to Flavia Sorichetti for her support.

Many thanks to all the faculty of the architecture section at ENAC, EPFL—in particular Sarah Nichols, Stefana Parascho, Jo Taillieu, Sophie Delhay, Pier Vittorio Aureli, Marilyne Anderson, Jeffrey Huang, and Dieter Dietz—for their collegial support.

Image Credits

© Davide Broggio, Valentina Nadwornicek, Sofia Vila Clavell: 11
© Eva Oustric: 12
© Don McPhedran, Photographic Agency, via the State Library: 13
© Charlotte Malterre-Barthes: 14
© Foreign Architects Switzerland: 29
© Vitruvius Grind: 33
© FAECT *Bulletin* headlines, collected by Joshua Barnett, Adare Brown, James Heard, Jack Rusk, and the Alternative Building Industry Collective: 36
© Namita Vijay Dharia: 53, 55
© Carolina Pichler and Lalie Porteret: 68, 69, 73, 74
© Usina-CTAH and Pedro Fiori Arantes: 94, 95, 96, 102, 104

Every effort has been made by the authors and the publisher to acknowledge all sources and copyright holders. In the event of any copyright holder being inadvertently omitted, please contact the editor directly.

Impact Evaluation

	Carbon ($kg\ CO_2$)
Digital (computer utilization in communication with authors, editing, graphic design, copyediting, project management, lithography, communication with printer, marketing, distribution)	19
Test printing	0.16
Printing and binding (paper transport, interior paper, cover paper, ink, energy, glue, wrap)	540.46
Total	559.62
Total per copy	0.60

Colophon

Editor: Charlotte Malterre-Barthes
Managing editor: Kathlyn Kao
Editorial management: Lydia Fuchs
Copyediting: Irene Schaudies
Translations: Annabella Blyth
Graphic design: Fernanda Tellez Velasco
Reproductions: DLG Graphic, Paris
Production: Alise Ausmane
Paper: Salzer EOS 1.75, 80 g/m²
Printing and binding: H. Heenemann GmbH & Co. KG

Published by
Hatje Cantz Verlag GmbH
Mommsenstraße 27
10629 Berlin
Germany
contact@hatjecantz.de
www.hatjecantz.com
A Ganske Publishing Group Company

ISBN: 978-3-7757-6065-2 (Print)
ISBN: 978-3-7757-6066-9 (E-Book)

Printed in Germany

EPFL RIOT TU berlin